PUB W

JACK STREET

Ensign

First published in 1993 by
Ensign Publications
2 Redcar Street,
Southampton SO1 5LL.

a b c d

Publisher David Graves.
Designed by Precinct Press.
Cover by Design Laboratory.
Cover photo. by Terry Heathcote
Book photos. by Jack Street.
Maps by Jack Street.
Printed by Short Run Press, Exeter.

ISBN 185455 094 2

Walk · CONTENTS · Page

· INTRODUCTION ·

William Cobbett, that oft-quoted traveller and author of the English classic *Rural Rides*, wrote that 'those that travel on turnpike roads know nothing of England'. Those who walk England's footpaths and bridleways will fully endorse that statement and our fellow countrymen who drive hastily and eternally on motorways and trunk roads miss out on the true meaning and beauty of our pastoral countryside. As you wander along one of these remote footpaths you can enjoy the tranquillity of meadow and stream, admire the beauty of wild flowers, enjoy bird song or the rustle of a breeze in a woodland glade.

In the twenty walks I offer you in this book, there is a satisfying variety of landscapes to be enjoyed, from the pines of Windsor Forest to the beech-clad hangers and downlands of North-East Hampshire and the wild commons and heathlands of West Surrey. Central to this area and to the book, is the newly-cleansed Basingstoke Canal and the lure of walking beside its quiet waters, pleasant haunt of coot and moorhen. The sands and gravels of the Upper Blackwater Valley have provoked development and semi-urbanisation in the form of Camberley, Farnborough and Aldershot but even so, there are woodland and heathland enclaves which are fine for walking.

What better way to begin a countryside ramble than a drink and a meal at a good English pub. A blazing fire in winter, or a sun-shaded garden table in the summer, makes the perfect setting to relax you and put you in the right frame of mind for the walk ahead. Those inns I have recommended should fulfil your needs, provide a starting point for your walk and a place to leave your car — but do ask for permission first.

Many of the directions I have provided, to enable you to reach the starting point of each walk by car, will be affected by the new Blackwater Valley Route and the Runfold Diversion, both due to open in August 1994 and to supersede parts of the A325 and the A31. I can only apologise for this on behalf of the Department of Transport — the alternative would have been to delay this publication by a year!

Although most of the walks follow well-established paths, tracks and bridleways, there are sections which can be muddy and some paths which are not well-used. I suggest you equip yourself with good, strong waterproof footwear at all times and I advise against wearing shorts, as English nettles and brambles wreak havoc on unprotected legs! I personally find a walking stick comes in very handy. Finally and most importantly, please do observe the countryside code and help farmers, and other land owners, who are not the ogres they are sometimes made out to be. Secure all gates behind you, leave no litter, try and stay on the beaten path and if you have a dog, keep it under control.

JACK STREET
October 1993

National Trust lands & valley lakes from Finchampstead

WALK 1
Allow 4 hours
6 miles
Walk begins page 8

Background to the Walk

A little to the north of the winding River Blackwater, which acts as the County boundary between Hampshire and Berkshire, lies the pleasantly named village of Finchampstead. The village readily splits into two separate identities, the old part lying off the beaten track, clustered around the dominant church and the attractive, gabled Queens Oak pub, while the newer part scatters itself around better lines of communication centred around the Greyhound pub to the south. As is the case with many other villages in these parts, the area was originally part of the Royal Forest of Windsor enclosed in 1086 for the purpose of hunting deer and wild boar. The Forest was divided into bailiwicks and Finchampstead formed one of these.

The village name derives from 'a homestead frequented by finches' and there are wild birds aplenty in the woods of Finchampstead Ridges and the Moor Green Lakes Nature Reserve nearby. The village was something of a backwater in earlier days and only the opening of Eversley Bridge in 1819 made the neighbourhood more accessible. The area around the fine church of St. James is still a backwater and hopefully it will remain so and retain its aura of peace and tranquillity. Access to the old village is by three country lanes which converge pleasantly at the village green where you can find two special oak trees. As you approach the church, the tree to the left was planted in 1901 to commemorate Queen Victoria (The village pub takes its name from this, as formerly it was known as The White Horse Inn) and the other oak to the right dates from 1935 to commemorate the Silver Jubilee of King

Maps
Landranger 1:50,000
Sheet 186
Pathfinder 1:25,000
Sheets 1188 SU66/76
and 1189 SU86/96.
Map Reference of Start/
Finish SU793639

How to get there
From Farnham take A325 to Farnborough and then take A327 left handed from the roundabout eventually passing over junction 4A with M3. Continue north to A30 turning left to follow this for 2 miles then turning right to resume A327 towards Reading. Take first right (signed Eversley Cross) and proceed to Finchampstead. At the top end of the village, by Greyhound pub, turn right on to B3348 (signed Crowthorne). Take the first turn left (Church Lane) signposted Finchampstead Church and follow the lane to the green and the Queens Oak. From Camberley take A30 to Yorktown turning right on to A321 through Sandhurst to the junction with B3348. Turn left here and continue for over a mile, then looking out for Church Lane on the right signposted to Finchampstead Church. Follow this to the green and the Queens Oak. Reading Bus

Service no 141 operates between Yateley and Wokingham via Eversley Cross and Finchampstead. It would be advisable to alight at the Greyhound in the village and join the walk at that point. Check bus times on 0734 509509 (Reading Buses). From Farnham take one of several services to Aldershot Bus Station and change to Stagecoach Service 20 or 20A to Yateley. From Camberley there is a choice of several services to Yateley including 25, 430 and 444 (Stagecoach) and F22 (Tillingbourne).

**Pub facilities
Queens Oak,
Finchampstead**

This fine white fronted, multi gabled pub stands facing the green with the village church on the hill close by. Church and pub have a connection, for when the Victorians restored the church, the old church porch was acquired by the pub to enhance its gabled aspect. A friendly, pleasing brick-faced bar welcomes the visitor as you enter by the left-hand door and your attention will soon be riveted by the amazing collection of 1500 key fobs over and around the bar. You can drink in the long main bar or retire to the snug (no smoking) bar on the left, both serving Brakspear's Bitter, Old Ale and Special. There are no guest ales but lagers, cider and stout are available between the hours of 11.30-14.30 (16.00 in the summer) and 18.00-23.00 with the normal 12.00-15.00 and 19.00-22.30 on Sundays. When we called, the pub only provided pizzas (but many of them) and ploughmans, but

The Queen's Oak at Finchampstead

George V. The church, standing rather massively on its hill, retains the walls of the original structure which dates from the Conquest or possibly earlier. The eastern end of the chancel is apsidal or semi-circular which is an unusual feature in English churches. The font, however, may well be the oldest part of the church and is probably the original font taken from the older church dating from circa 1030. The brick tower was erected in 1720 and contains six bells, five of which were installed in 1792 and the sixth added in 1885 to commemorate the 80th birthday of the rector, the Reverend Edward St. John.

John Walter of Bear Wood to the north, played a part in the development of the area, particularly at Finchampstead Ridges which are on the walk route. These form an outlier of the sandy Upper Bagshot geological Beds whose soft structure has been preserved by a capping of gravel (a similar feature to the hill on which Finchampstead church stands). Pine, silver birch, sweet chestnut and rhododendrons thrive on the well drained acid soil of the Ridges. John Walter was a Berkshire MP and a proprietor of *The Times* newspaper. The Ridges formed part of his Bear Wood estate and in 1863 he had a road constructed on top of the Ridges. Six years later he planted an avenue of Wellingtonia trees along the new road. Sources say that this was done to commemorate Waterloo which took

The Greyhound at Finchampstead

things are to change very soon
and a full, varied menu will be
on offer between the hours of
12.00-14.00 and 19.00-22.00
(Mon-Sat), 12.00-14.00 and
19.00-21.30 on Sundays. The
present multiple choice of
pizzas (large and small) will
remain. There is a large
garden to the side with picnic
tables and a log fort for
children. Tel. 0734 734855.
Walkers may leave their cars
in the ample car park after
first asking permission.

Greyhound, Finchampstead

This pub is more of a road
house standing at the upper
end of the newer village. A
Brewer's Fayre pub, it is
popular, busy and festooned
with window boxes and
hanging baskets. It is
Victorian-looking inside with
a picture rail and floral
wallpaper. You can eat in the
bar or restaurant between
11.30-22.00 (Mon-Sat) and
12.00-22.30 (Sun) from the
Brewers Fayre menu or the
blackboard specials like
Sunday roasts, macaroni
cheese or mushroom and nut
fettucini. Drinks on offer
included Brakspear,
Boddingtons, Flowers
Original and Whitbread Best
ales served up between 11.00-
23.00 (Mon-Sat) 12.00-15.00
and 19.00-22.30 (Sun). There
is a garden at the front with a
childrens' play area. Tel 0734
732305. Car parking space is
ample and walkers may leave
their cars with permission.

place 54 years earlier and that you could stand at the eastern end of Wellingtonia Avenue and see Wellington's home at Stratfield Saye House seven miles away. This story may be as tall as the 150ft high avenue of Wellingtonias, as Bramshill Forest stands in the line of vision. Wellingtonias can reach a height of 350ft and live 4000 years in their native habitat on the Pacific coast of the USA, but it is unlikely that these fine specimens will reach that height or live that long. The area of Finchampstead Ridges are now in the care of the National Trust. A public subscription of £3000 purchased the first 60 acres of the Ridges for the Trust in 1913 and in recent years this has increased to 138 acres.

The walk passes through the Moor Green Lakes Nature Reserve which is a haven for wildfowl and well noted for its wintering and breeding birds — amongst the latter group are plovers, redshanks, tern and lapwing. The lakes are the result of gravel extraction between the mid seventies and 1992 by Hall Aggregates who own the site. A local committee set up by Halls and the Blackwater Valley Management Service looks after the area and many improvements are planned including the provision of viewing hides.

Further gravel workings are planned to the west to the annoyance of residents in the Cricket Hill area of Finchampstead. Horseshoe Lake, so called because it has an island of that shape, has been scheduled for water sport activities such as wind surfing, canoeing and dinghy sailing.

Walk 1

Distance: *Allow a good four hours for this walk of six miles*

From the Queens Oak, turn left and head down the lane past Church Farm looking out for a stile and a footpath sign on your left. Go obliquely right on a well defined meadow path to a stile in the far corner of the field. Cross this and the lane, crossing another stile a little to the left and walk up the right hand side of a field to a wooden kissing gate in the top corner. There is a metal seat on the left from which you can admire the view back to Finchampstead Church on its hill with houses grouped below. A truly English scene.

A confined path now leads up to the tarmac access road to Warren Crest Farm. Go left handed on this until you meet a track where you turn right and when it ceases by Keepers Cottage, carry on along a wooded path which soon reverts to track status serving houses to your left. Oak, sweet chestnut and birch shade your way until you meet a metalled access road where you turn right to where the road ends by the fine, imperious looking wrought iron gates of Willow Wick Farm. After comparing these with your own front gates, proceed ahead past a bridleway sign and follow a pleasant, sandy path through woodland up to Tudor Cottage on your right, together with other residential buildings once known as Ridge Farm. Continue on the track until you reach the Finchampstead — Crowthorne road which you cross with care to join Dell Road opposite.

Remain on Dell Road as it swoops and twists through wooded country with scattered housing. Shortly after passing several houses on the left, the road swings right-handed with woodland on the left replacing the houses. Where a straight track goes left soon after the bend, leave the road and join this track leading east through fine woodland with a wire fence usually visible to your right. You reach Spout Pond on your left shortly after the track has narrowed to a path between an oak tree and holly bushes. Blue dragonflies hovered above the water as we rested awhile and a few water lilies shyly peeped through their foliage to enjoy the warm summer sun. This area is part of National Trust property called Finchampstead Ridges and you will see a sign announcing this as you continue ahead and then veer right past a barrier on to a track. Turn left to pass a sign announcing Rorkes Drift with a fox surmounting the sign and horse paddocks beyond. Leave this reminder of the Zulu wars behind and follow a pleasant, shaded track climbing up through mixed woodland with a woody valley on the right. Look out for a path turning right as you pass over an abrupt summit. The burned out remains of a car littered the path junction when we passed and I hope this eyesore has been removed before you pass this spot.

Turn right on to the path and enjoy walking through ridge top beech woodland, remaining on the main path and ignoring all paths leading right. The path becomes narrow in places with a profusion of brambles and heads downhill past a couple of marker posts. Meadowland appears on each side before a right hand bend in the path takes you down past woods on your left and the tree crowned Beech Hill on your right. Soon you join a track from the right which you follow left

Walk 1

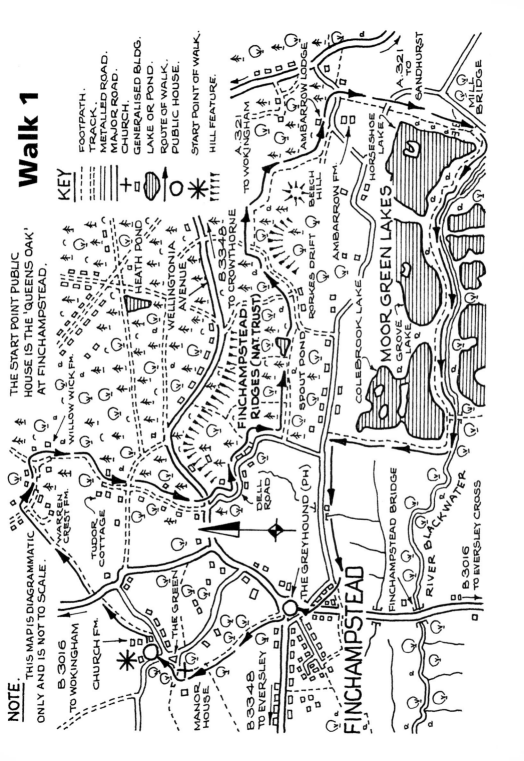

KEY

- – – – – FOOTPATH.
- ------- TRACK.
- ═══════ METALLED ROAD.
- ━━━━━━━ MAJOR ROAD.
- ✝ CHURCH.
- ⬭ GENERALISED BLDG.
- ◑ LAKE OR POND.
- ○ LAKE OR POND.
- ➤ ROUTE OF WALK.
- ⬭ PUBLIC HOUSE.
- ✳ START POINT OF WALK.
- ⟋⟋⟋ HILL FEATURE.

NOTE. THIS MAP IS DIAGRAMMATIC ONLY AND IS NOT TO SCALE.

THE START POINT PUBLIC HOUSE IS THE 'QUEENS OAK' AT FINCHAMPSTEAD.

B 3016 TO WOKINGHAM

CHURCH FM.

WARREN CREST FM.

TUDOR COTTAGE

WILLOW WICK FM.

HEATH POND

WELLINGTONIA AVENUE

B 3348 TO CROWTHORNE

RIDGES (NAT. TRUST)

FINCHAMPSTEAD

DELL ROAD

SPOUT POND

RORKES DRIFT

BEECH HILL

A. 321 TO WOKINGHAM

AMBARROW LODGE

AMBARROW FM.

HORSESHOE LAKE

A. 321 TO SANDHURST

MILL BRIDGE

COLEBROOK LAKE

GROVE LAKE

MOOR GREEN LAKES

THE GREEN

MANOR HOUSE

THE GREYHOUND (PH)

B 3348 TO EVERSLEY

FINCHAMPSTEAD

FINCHAMPSTEAD BRIDGE

RIVER BLACKWATER

B 3016 TO EVERSLEY CROSS

B 3016 TO WOKINGHAM

St James, Finchampstead

handed to a metal gate, passing it left-handed and then turning left on to the road beyond. As you do this, look left and admire the black and white gabled Ambarrow Lodge with its attendant rambler roses. Just before the lane bends left, take a signed path on the right, through a kissing gate and alongside the right-hand edge of two consecutive meadows until you meet a road by way of a wooden kissing gate. A two-armed footpath sign directs you across the road and through another kissing gate.

You now enter the area of Moor Green Lakes Nature Reserve. The gravel extraction pits of yesteryear have been turned into a series of lakes stretching along the course of the River Blackwater. Follow the well-defined path forward alongside the water to cross a planked footbridge and continue on a boardwalk. Where this divides, take the right hand fork up to a kissing gate and join the riverside path. Turn right and follow the path between lakes and river for nearly one mile. We saw the occasional languid fisherman trying his luck in the river and a flotilla of Canada Geese lazed in one of the lakes to the right. Shortly after a path from Yateley joins from a left-hand footbridge, the path you are following strikes north to meet the Lower Sandhurst Road by the side of a car park. Over the latter part of this section there are two parallel paths — you can use either of these. Turn left and follow the lane to Finchampstead turning right with the road as it meets the houses. At the top of Cricket Hill, turn right at the cross roads and go past the Greyhound pub (unless you want to call in for refreshment!) to the road junction at the far end of the pub car park. Turn left here and quickly look for an access on the right with a footpath sign set well back from the road. The path from here up to Finchampstead Church is one of the best parts of the walk as you gently rise up past the sports ground. If you want to sit down and enjoy the view there is a Silver Jubilee metal seat for four by the pathside. Soon the church's brick tower can be seen between the trees and you enter the churchyard through a wooden kissing gate. The massive, buttressed church tower dominates the churchyard and certainly St. James is worth a visit. The church has earlier origins but it took its present form in 1150. Leaving the church, pass down through the wooden gate keeping to the left of the green back to the Queens Oak.

10,000 pines and the Devil's highway from Bagshot

WALK 2
Allow 4 hours
6 ½ miles
Walk begins page 13

Background to the Walk

The Royal hunting Forest of Windsor at one time enveloped the whole of Bagshot and spread its sylvan glades southwards to include Pirbright and Farnborough. 2,600 acres of the Forest remain basically as it was hundreds of years ago, although husbandry by the Crown Estate may be a little more intense. The Crown Estate owns more than 250,000 acres in England, Scotland and Wales and its origins date from the 11th century. Until the time of George III, the Sovereign enjoyed rents and profits from these lands but after that profits were surrendered to Parliament under provision of the Civil List. The original Forest of Windsor was enclosed in 1086 and was managed for the hunting of deer and wild boar for the King and his friends.

Bagshot was a staging post astride the London to Exeter road and boasted 14 inns for travellers. As with many heathlands, the area was infested with highwaymen — Dick Turpin, Parson Darby, the Golden Farmer and Claude Duval amongst them. Bagshot Heath was a favourite haunt for these gentlemen of the road and William Cobbett described it as 'a villainous place'. In an agricultural sense, Defoe said that the Heath was 'not only good for little, but good for nothing'. The Romans dared to cross the area with a road between Silchester and Staines which later became known as 'The Devils Highway'. The Devil has had his name attached to many similar features, due largely to the fears and suspicions of country folk of long ago. Following the collapse of the Roman Empire in the 5th Century, this road survived as a superb example of

Maps
Landranger 1:50,000
Sheet 186
Pathfinder 1:25,000
Sheet 1189 SU86/96
Map Reference of Start/
Finish SU906626

How to get there
From Farnham follow A325 through Farnborough and Frimley to join A30 at the Jolly Farmer pub. Turn right and continue towards Bagshot. The Bird in Hand is on your left as you descend the hill into Bagshot. From Camberley simply follow A30 towards Bagshot and look for the pub as above. Buses between Camberley Station and Bagshot Square are frequent including 34, 35 and 584 (Guildford and West Surrey) and 500 (Dickson's Travel). From Farnham, Tillingbourne Bus Co service no. F40 operates on a two-hourly basis between Farnham and Camberley stations. There are other services but you will need to change at Aldershot Bus station.

Pub facilities
Bird In Hand,
Bagshot

David and Teresa Kennard have administered this Free House for over a year now and are set upon improving its image. There is a welcome notice over the saloon bar which sets a good tone. There is romance in the air here as David and Teresa first met some years ago at the pub. They married, moved away from the area and now have returned in style. A restaurant to the left with green patterned carpet and deep red velvet curtains seats 20. The public bar with pool table lies to the right. Courage Best and Websters Yorkshire Bitter can be sampled during opening hours 11.00-15.00 and 17.30-23.00 (Mon-Sat) with normal Sunday opening times (12.00-15.00, 19.00-22.30). If its food you are after, the menu is extensive, ranging from Tandoori Chicken to a T bone steak for the main course with fish dishes and a fine range of sandwiches, ploughmans and salads. Your appetite can be satisfied between the hours of 12.00-14.00 and 18.00-21.00 (or 21.30) (Mon-Sat) and 12.00-14.00 on Sundays when roasts are served. Picnic benches line the forecourt and there is good car parking where walkers may leave their vehicles with permission. The ladies toilet is rather special with powder and perfume available for free use and even a few cuddly bears dotted around. Tel 0276 475554.

The Bird in Hand at Bagshot

their civil engineering skills. To the primitive folk who followed the Romans and had no comparable skills, a road of this perfection was viewed with awe, and hushed voices proclaimed that the Devil himself had built it.

Bagshot is not far away from the Royal Castle of Windsor and Royalty has featured strongly in its history. The coming of the railways before 1850 meant that the village suffered a depression in its trade as a staging post. The third son of Queen Victoria, born in 1850, played a great part in the revival of the village. Prince Arthur was created Duke of Connaught in 1874 and five years later married Princess Louise Marguerite of Prussia. Just to the north of the village was the fine house of Bagshotpark set in parkland splendour which had been the home of the Duke of Gloucester, brother of George III. After his death, the house fell vacant and Victoria, seeking a wedding present for Arthur, had the old house demolished and a grand new one built. The Duke of Connaught and his new bride moved into the modern mansion in 1880. He always said that he was a resident of the village and consequently had much involvement in village affairs and local issues. He had a fine Army career and was Governor General of Canada from 1911-1916. He died at Bagshot in 1942 thus ending a 62-year link with the village.

Fighting Cocks, Kings Arms and **The Three Mariners**
These three are High Street pubs all serving good food. The Three Mariners has no connection with the sea but is of great age dating back some 600 years. An old haunt for highwaymen operating on Bagshot Heath, the pub contains a fine wooden gallery and is full of old timbers.

Left: The Three Mariners, Bagshot

The parish church of St. Annes replaced the former St. Annes Chapel in School Lane. In 1874, Bagshot, formerly in the parish of Windlesham, became a separate parish. The foundation stone of the new church was laid by the Duke of Connaught in 1883 after giving the land from his estate and contributing £300 to the cost. The new church was consecrated by the Bishop of Winchester in April 1884. The church, which you pass on the walk (see picture page 16), is an impressive brick structure with a slender attractive spire which can be seen over the trees for miles around. The Royal tradition of Bagshot has been maintained by the Queen Mother, who visited the church in 1984 and 1990, the latter visit being to unveil a plaque in the church to Sir Alexander and Lady Patricia Ramsay (a daughter of the Duke and Duchess of Connaught).

No word about Bagshot is complete without a mention of Waterer's Nursery which has for so long occupied its site on Jenkins Hill, the entrance being directly opposite to the Bird in Hand pub. In 1828, Michael Waterer of Knaphill bought John Taylor's nursery, which was inherited by brother John in 1842 and by 1856 had expanded to 100 acres. He was followed, in turn, by his son, also called John who was a colourful character and did much to help in the village and became the largest employer of labour in the neighbourhood. The nursery has since been taken over by Nottcutts, but the Waterer name survives.

Walk 2
Distance: *Allow at least four hours for this walk of six-and-a-half miles*
Leave the pub to walk left-handed down the main road, past the pelican crossing, then turning left into Church Road. An old drinking trough on the corner asks you to 'be kind to all God's creatures'. With this resolution in mind, proceed uphill and past the Victorian Church of St. Annes which is normally locked, although you can acquire a key from the vicarage next door. The next turning right is Vicarage Road, which your route follows and continues after the metalling ends on a wooded

undulating and at times muddy track. Continue directly ahead on this track, which changes its name to Vicarage Lane well before you arrive at a metal gate with an adjacent kissing gate. Woodland eases back as you are confronted by two tracks going straight ahead in parallel. Take the right-hand one passing under a sweet chestnut tree. These trees favour a porous, acid soil and were probably introduced into Britain by the Romans. It is indigenous to Spain (sometimes called the Spanish chestnut) and used in the manufacture of castanets (from its generic name Castanea). You will see a number of these trees on the walk.

Sign at Upper Star Post

Pines and bracken dominate as you reach a T-junction of tracks, with the parallel track on the left merging in also. Turn left on the uphill track and soon reach a Windsor Forest sign post at a track crossing. Proceed right-handed which is signed Old Bracknell Road and Look Out. With the fresh scent of pine in the air, continue to where a track branches left shortly before a sharp incline. Divert on to this track and climb quite steeply up through pines which were being thinned out as we passed and as you curve gently right a fine view of the undulating track unfolds in front of you, culminating in a severe climb at the far end on the flanks of New England Hill. When you have toiled to the top, look back to a sea of pines seemingly stretching on forever. Having recovered your stamina, proceed and go left as you reach a track junction on to a pleasant, woodland route which takes you over a track crossing to another cross track, where you turn left by a Ramblers Route wooden marker post.

A wide track now takes you directly south westwards through predominantly pine woodland, past the mound of Crowthorne reservoir on your right, to the convergence of many tracks called Upper Star Post. This spot is also called Roman Star, as it stands on the line of the Roman road between Silchester and Staines called The Devil's Highway. Look along its route to the west over seemingly interminable heathland towards Crowthorne. A marker post gives a destination to all six routes radiating from the star. Take the track marked 'Redoubt' and 'Lower Star Post'. There are seven earthworks in the area called redoubts which are circular fortifications, built to train militiamen in 1792 when the threat of invasion by Napoleon Bonaparte hung over the land.

Lower Star Post is soon reached and is a convergence of even more tracks than at Upper Star. We counted ten, although a couple on the southern side carry warnings of a military firing range and one is fenced off. The area to the south west is the training ground for the Royal Military Academy at nearby Sandhurst. Take care on leaving this spot as the marker post is not so comprehensive as the one at

Walk 2

THE START POINT PUBLIC HOUSE
IS THE 'BIRD IN HAND' AT BAGSHOT.
KEY TO OTHER PUBLIC HOUSES:-
1. THE FIGHTING COCKS.
2. THE KINGS ARMS.
3. THE THREE MARINERS.

NOTE

THIS MAP IS DIAGRAMMATIC ONLY
AND IS NOT TO SCALE.

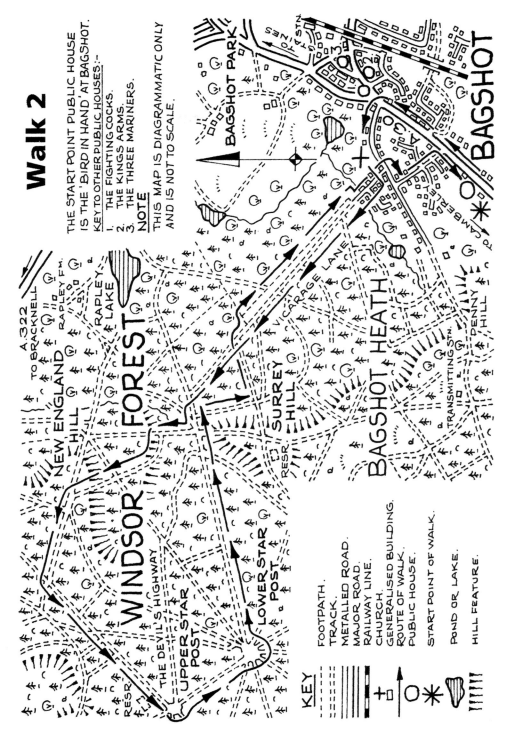

KEY

FOOTPATH.
TRACK.
METALLED ROAD.
MAJOR ROAD.
RAILWAY LINE.
CHURCH.
GENERALISED BUILDING.
ROUTE OF WALK.
PUBLIC HOUSE.

START POINT OF WALK.

POND OR LAKE.

HILL FEATURE.

Upper Star. Take the third exit on the left (actually called Lake Ride) which is the one to the left of the track bordered by electricity transmission lines. A sharp rise is followed by further undulations as you head straight along this track ignoring any side paths. Eventually you reach the top of a sharp incline which you descend and continue ahead as tracks join from left and right. Proceed to a crossing of tracks which you will remember from your outward route by the Windsor sign post. Carry straight on, ignoring a diverging track to the left until you reach a right turning track. Follow this over a wet hollow uphill to a track crossing under the shoulder of Surrey Hill to your right. Turn to your left downhill to meet a cross track at the bottom where you go right-handed towards the metal gate you passed on your outward journey. Cross over the intervening open ground to pass to the left of the

St Annes Church, Bagshot

gate and veer right immediately to pass under the canopies of two sweet chestnut trees backed by a Scots pine. Your track now parallels the fenced Vicarage Lane you used on the outward journey to the right. Continue on this undulating track through some wet areas keeping straight ahead on a lesser grassy track where the main track turns left. You are still parallel to Vicarage Lane as electricity pylons come in from the right and then take up the line of the route you are following. Very shortly after this, you will see a double wooden gate on your right and a wide gravel area to the left, where timber was stacked as we passed. To the left of the double gates, you will find a purpose made gap which you pass through and turn left to eventually meet Church Road again.

When you meet Church Road go right and then immediately left into Higgs Lane. If you feel like a sit-down hereabouts, there are a couple of wayside seats where you can rest. Suitably rested you then proceed down Higgs Lane and continue straight up to meet the main road where you turn right and back to the Bird in Hand.

Heather and gorse lands from Burrowhill

WALK 3
Allow 3 hours
5 miles
Walk begins page 19

Background to the Walk

As you travel north on B383 from the attractive Surrey village of Chobham, you soon arrive at Burrowhill without seeing any intervening open country, but you are pleasantly surprised when a village green opens up and forces the houses back to its fringes. This is Burrowhill Green and a line of houses and cottages, particularly on its western side, enhances its attraction. The Four Horseshoes pub sits picturesquely on this side and further down you will see the well established village blacksmith's forge and shop, now sympathetically modernised. This is the heart of Burrowhill, a name probably derived from Barrowhill, as seven barrows have been discovered in these parts and one is scheduled as an ancient monument.

Burrowhill lies on the southern fringe of Chobham Common, a typical area of Surrey heathland now bisected by the M3 motorway. It is managed by the Surrey County Council Countryside Service under the surveillance of Andy Wragg the Ranger. The common is dry heathland with much common heather (ling) and the attractively flowered bell heather, together with common and dwarf gorse. The lovely blue Marsh Gentian flourishes in poorly drained areas on the Common and the rare sand lizard and smooth snake are at home here. If you examine the OS Pathfinder map no. 1189, you will find evidence of former occupants of the Common at two locations, one in Albury Bottom and the other lying to the east of Gracious Pond, both described as a Bee Garden. There is a tale to tell here and strangely enough it begins in Chobham churchyard. Up to 1215, the Chobham's dead were taken to

Maps
Landranger 1:50,000
Sheet 186
Pathfinder 1:25,000
Sheet 1189 SU86/96
Map Reference of Start/
Finish SU970629

How to get there
From the large roundabout on the A31 east of Farnham, follow A324 through Ash and Pirbright to Brookwood where you join A322 northbound over the canal bridge. Take the second turning right (signed Chobham) and proceed to Chobham joining B383 and then A319. Follow A319 right-handed, but where this road turns sharply right, continue straight ahead on B383 to Burrowhill. The Four Horseshoes lies over the green to your left. From Camberley take A30 eastwards and at The Jolly Farmer turn right to join B3015, crossing the motorway to Heatherside Corner where you turn left and follow B311 (Red Road) to the roundabout, where you cross A322 and proceed straight ahead on A319 to Chobham. Where A319 turns sharply right, follow B383 straight ahead to Burrowhill. Guildford and West Surrey regular service No. 539 runs between Woking Station and Bowling Green Road in North Chobham. If

you alight here, it is less than a quarter mile along Windsor Road to the Four Horseshoes on Burrowhill Green. My advice is to travel by British Rail from Farnham and Camberley to Woking Station and join service 539 there. Dickson Travel service 500 provides a very limited alternative from Camberley on three days a week to Burrowhill. Check on 0252 344083 if you wish to use this route.

Pub facilities
Four Horseshoes,
Burrowhill Green
Standing on the west side of Burrowhill Green, the pub forms an attractive setting, half hidden by a yew tree with hanging baskets ablaze with impatiens and fuchsias. A tarmac forecourt fronts this whitewashed brick pub. Speak it softly, but years ago before it became a pub, part of it served as a mortuary and predictably the spectre of a man in a top hat is said to walk from that direction! The pub has a lease from Courage and serves Courage Best, Morlands Old Speckled Hen and Brakspear Bitter. If you fancy lager, you can sample Fosters, Carlsberg, Kronenburg or alcohol free Kalibur. All these, together with cider and wines, can be enjoyed between the hours of 11.00-15.00 and 17.30-23.00 (Mon - Sat) and Sundays between 12.00-15.00 and 19.00-22.30. If you wish to eat, there is a printed menu and a specials board with Steaks, Mexican Chilli, Chicken Kiev and Lasagnes on the former, and potato, egg and mushroom cheesy bake or Tandoori Kebabs on the latter.

The Four Horseshoes at Burrowhill Green

Chertsey, all of six miles away for burial. This of course was not very convenient so a petition was finally sent to Pope Honorious for permission to bury them in a graveyard around the church. The Pope granted this, subject to Chertsey Abbey receiving 10 lbs of beeswax a year and a bee farm was established on Chobham Common to fulfil this condition.

Pomp and ceremony came to the Common on 21 June 1853 when a grand military camp was set up there for Queen Victoria to review her troops in company with Albert, the Prince Consort prior to the troops' departure to fight the Crimean War. Actually the camp was held from April to August so that officers could learn to command large bodies of men and at the same time, learn how to survive in a field camp. This was considered such a success that a permanent base for the Army was sought and in 1854 Aldershot was selected as the home of the British Army. When Queen Victoria died in 1901 a monument was erected on that part of Chobham Common (north of the M3) to commemorate the grand gathering of the Army in 1853 and the Queen's review.

The village of Chobham lies to the south in the shallow valley of the Mill Bourne, whose waters feed the Wey to the east. The ancient village church, dedicated to St. Lawrence, dates from 1080 with the buttressed tower being built circa 1400. At the foot of the

The Chobham Forge at Burrowhill

These are but a small selection from a wide ranging choice. Enjoy the food between 12.00-14.00 and 19.00-22.00 (Mon - Fri), 12.00-14.30 and 19.00-22.00 (Sat), 12.00-14.30 and 19.00-21.00 (Sun). There are tables and benches on the forecourt and many small bar areas inside the pub ranging from the public bar with a pool table, a cosy little snug bar and a sectioned large saloon bar. Seating is ample with wall seats, tables and chairs. Children are allowed in the bar and there is car parking to front, side and rear. Walkers may leave cars with permission. When I visited, new tenants were due to take over very shortly, and it is hoped that the pub's good atmosphere will continue. Tel 0276 857581.

sanctuary step is buried Archbishop Heath, who proclaimed Elizabeth Tudor as Queen in 1558 following the disastrous reign of Mary. The font has a special antiquity, as it is octagonal and made of wood dating from the 16th Century. There are only three wooden fonts of this age in the country.

Walk 3

Distance: *Allow three hours for this walk of five miles*

Leave the pub and take the road which leads obliquely left over the green to cross Windsor Road and enter Gorse Lane opposite. If you glance back, you will be treated to a pleasant village green scene before you proceed to join Heather Way, which leaves Gorse Lane as the latter turns right-handed. This is a narrow residential lane which soon meets a track where you turn right and follow it as it curves to the left. Oak and birch shade your route until you meet another track where you turn left and then almost immediately right to join a side path. Wend your way through silver birch, gorse and bracken, passing underneath transmission lines and cross first a path and then a gravel track. Your path is a pleasant one on the western fringe of Chobham Common, although a car dump visible through trees on your right mars the scene. Avert your eyes and soon reach a track joining from your left where you turn right past a vehicle barrier to join the access track to the car dump. Turn left and follow this track past a picturesque cottage to meet the Burrowhill to Longcross road. Cross straight over, ignoring a path which branches left and follow the wider path uphill with open common land to your right. Chobham Common is the haunt of the silver studded blue butterfly so look out on the walk for this lovely specimen. I was lucky enough to see two of the species fluttering around together.

As your path rises towards the quaintly named Chickabiddy Hill, good views open up over the common to your right. A path joins yours from the left before you bend right under a low voltage transmission line to pass a stagnant heathland pool on your left. The pretty, blue Marsh Gentian blooms in these parts so look out for these flowers as well as the butterflies. Just after the pool, ignore a track branching left and make your way to a crossing of tracks. The inauspicious Chickabiddy Hill lies directly ahead but you turn right and follow the track over fairly open common land until you reach a car park. An information panel lies on the far side if you would like to know more about Chobham Common.

Leave the car park by the height controlled exit and cross the road to locate a track parallel to the road alignment. Turn left on this and make your way along the ridge of Staple Hill with good views over the heather clad Albury Bottom on your right. Gorse, common heather, and the pretty flowered bell heather are your companions, although a less welcome companion is the constant roar of traffic on the M3, fortunately out of sight to your left. Soon you meet a T junction of tracks where you turn right, keeping left shortly ahead as the track divides. Go left again as the track soon divides into three by a lone pine in an island formed by the track junction. A shady section of the walk now follows with the fresh scent of pines in the air. This track forms the northern perimeter of Chobham Common and you will see a fence through the trees on your left. Bagshot Sands give a loose, sandy top soil and you encounter much deep sand, which is churned up by horses and forcing you to walk at the edges — a prime reason why these paths tend to become ever wider. As you meet another track, turn left and see a possible solution to the problem in the way of a laid carpet of wood shavings, which give a firmer base for horses and walkers alike.

Another heathland pond lies to your right before you turn right uphill at a track junction. Where the track forks at the top of the brief hill, take the one leading left which becomes very sandy as you pass under transmission lines. Keep ahead into a close set pine plantation ignoring all side turnings. Where your route veers right, turn with it as the trees relax their grip to give open heather clad heathland on the left. Pines and birch re-assert themselves as your track takes a left-hand curve followed by a sharper right-hand curve. Shortly after this, look for a two wheeled track forking left to join another coming in from the right. Follow a shaded, muddy track until you meet a lane.

Follow this lane left-handed, looking out for a footpath sign on the right shortly before the lane bends left. Pass a vehicle barrier and follow a woodland track until it turns slightly left to enter an area called the Fishpool Triangle. Your route lies along the signed footpath through barriers on the right which leads you through pleasant, deciduous woodland — a total contrast to the earlier common lands. All too soon this path reaches a horse barrier and joins a muddy track which you follow right-handed. Shortly, you will see a path branching left and it is worth deviating here to the banks of a limpid, water lily clad pool. At a place like this, on a warm sunny afternoon, time stands still. With an effort, free yourself from the

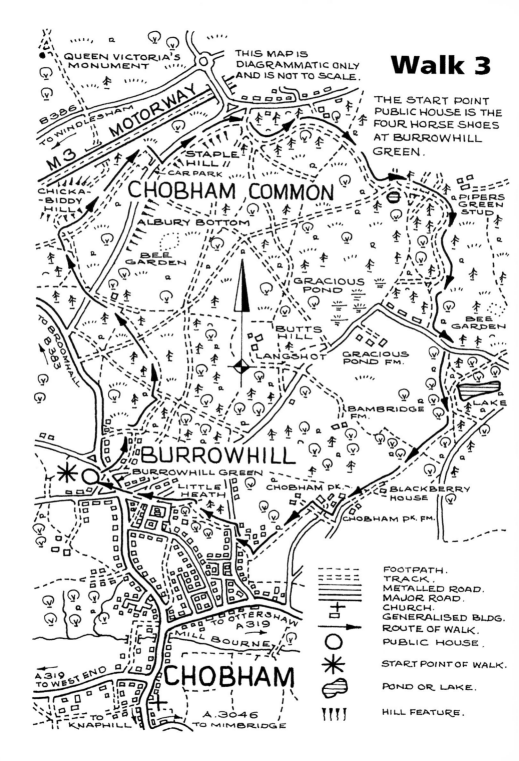

spell and return to the track which you follow until it veers left. At this point keep straight ahead through barriers beneath oak and birch canopies until you see a path branching right. Take this fenced path alongside dog kennels to a stile which you cross and follow a defined path over meadowland, keeping to the right of a solitary horse chestnut tree until you reach the

Tranquil pond near Stonehill

left-hand corner of woodland. Here you will find a leaning, three armed signpost and keeping the woodland on your right, cross two stiles and then with a fence on your right cross two further stiles as you proceed straight ahead to join a wide, fenced farm track.

Carry on past Blackberry House and continue through the yard of Chobham Park Farm on a concrete road. Pass through and close the white gate behind you. Shortly after the gate, look for a footpath sign (Path No 52) which points your way right along a track to a wooden gate. Pass to the left of this and proceed over the ostentatious entrance to Chobham Park House. Just beyond this, cross a stile on your left and at right angles to your former direction, follow a defined path over a meadow to a stepless stile and continue on the same alignment over another meadow to a further stepless stile to the left of a line of trees. Maintain your direction with a hedge to your right down to the field corner by a small pony paddock where you will find another stile, this time with a step. Cross over and follow a confined path right-handed behind houses until you emerge at a road junction opposite to a magnificent Chilean pine (or monkey puzzle tree) in the garden of a bungalow.

Cross over the side road called The Avenue and continue ahead until a track branches left opposite to a white house called Tree Tops. Follow the track which is signed as a footpath and continue alongside Little Heath, which is an area of trees and grassland, until you see the gates of a house ahead. Here you will perceive a well trodden grassy footpath heading off to the right. Follow this and take the main path which veers into the trees and over a footbridge to meet another path which joins from the right. Go left and soon you reach a metalled road called Little Heath Road. Follow this to eventually cross Windsor Road and the Four Horseshoes comes into view across the green obliquely right.

A lonely church and shaded waters from Knaphill

Background to the Walk

If you look at a map, you will find that Knaphill lies to the west of Woking, with its southern flank resting on the banks of the Basingstoke Canal. It appears to be something of a sprawl which is not uncommon in this part of Surrey, where many villages have expanded into a kind of rural suburbia. The name simply means 'the hill' and in the 13th Century it was known as 'La Cnappe' becoming 'Knephull' in the 15th Century. Appropriately, the centre of the village is on the top of Anchor Hill, which also housed the brickworks which provided building materials locally and also supplied bricks for building work on the Surrey section of the New Haw to Basingstoke Canal — opened in 1796.

The brickworks finally closed in 1925 after 135 years. It also provided bricks for the construction of Brookwood Hospital which lies within the built-up area of Knaphill. The hospital was established in 1867 as an asylum for what were referred to at the time as 'pauper lunatics'. On the eastern side of Knaphill, our walk takes us along an old route called the Barrack Path and you will see residential roads called Inkerman Way and Inkerman Road. These names commemorate the former Inkerman Barracks built of Knaphill bricks in the 19th Century. The buildings did not begin life as a barracks as they were originally constructed as male and female prisons. It was only in 1895 that the men's prison was converted to a barracks and in 1899 the adjacent women's prison followed suit. The barracks finally closed in 1965 and still remaining, is a fine terrace of 30 cottages with porches and gabled upper windows called Wellington Terrace.

Maps
Landranger 1:50,000
Sheet 186
Pathfinder 1:25,000
Sheet 1205 SU85/95
Map Reference of Start/
Finish SU958574

How to get there
From the large roundabout east of Farnham follow A324 through Ash and Pirbright to Brookwood traffic lights where you join A322 northbound over the canal bridge. The Hunters Lodge lies on your left-hand side. From Camberley take A321 southbound to Frimley Green where you turn left on to B3012 at the double mini roundabout. Follow B3012 to meet A324 at the railway arch where you follow A324 left-handed under the arch and continue along Connaught Road to meet A322 at the traffic lights. Turn left over the canal bridge and the Hunters Lodge soon appears on your left. From Farnham, the best route would be by British Rail from Farnham to Brookwood. Alight at Brookwood Station and take Connaught Road right-handed walking up to the traffic lights and turning left over the canal bridge, past the garage and up to Hunters Lodge on your left. The walking distance is a little

over half a mile. From Camberley, Guildford and West Surrey services 34, 35, 574 and 584 run to Woking via Knaphill Post Office which is a little over half a mile walk past Brookwood Hospital to the Hunters Lodge. Alternatively you could alight from these regular services at the Fox Inn on Guildford Road and begin the walk there. Guildford and West Surrey regular service 554 does pass the Hunters Lodge but the service would need to be joined at Frimley Green (Rose and Thistle) by way of regular Stagecoach services 549 and 550 from Camberley Station.

Pub facilities
Hunters Lodge,
Knaphill
Formerly called The Nags Head, this 19th century pub lay derelict for two years before re-opening in April 1993. A cream washed facade is enhanced by flower pots and hanging baskets and inside artificial plants drape over the attractive dark stained wooden bar. Piped music is subdued and pleasant and there are no fruit machines. A regal looking carpet gives the pub a quiet character. Opening times are 11.00-15.00 and 17 30-23.00 (Mon-Fri), 11.00-15.00 and 18.00-23.00 (Sat), 12.00-15.00 and 19.00-22.30 (Sun). It is a free house and you can enjoy Wadworth 6X, Ansells Bitter and Mild, Fullers London Pride and Tetley Bitter. Lowenbrau and Castlemaine Draught will satisfy lager drinkers. Food is prepared in a spotless kitchen by Mum between 12.00-14.30 and 18.00 (19.00 on Sun)-21.00 each day. A giant Yorkshire pudding filled with

The Hunters Lodge at Knaphill

Mention has already been made of Brookwood which is probably better known than Knaphill. Brookwood Cemetery is well known nationally and covers 400 acres of former heathland. An act of Parliament established this burial ground in 1854 to ease the pressure on London cemeteries and a special branch railway line was constructed to serve it from the main line at Brookwood. The relatively small community of Brookwood has a main line station and the Basingstoke Canal, which is on the walk route, fringes the village on its northern side.

The third village involved in this walk is Bisley, another semi-urbanised community whose centre has shifted westwards to straddle the main Bagshot to Guildford road from its origins by the lonely, ancient church of St. John the Baptist. Not far across the field from the church is a holy well, which by tradition, was a place where children were baptised in water that maintains a fairly constant temperature in summer and winter.

The crackle of small arms fire is synonymous with the name of Bisley and the world famous ranges lie to the south west of the village. Home of the National Rifle Association, the ranges play host to the world's top marksmen. Following the end of the Crimean War in 1856, the former allies became suspicious of each other and the stronger French Army was viewed with apprehension here. There were calls for a volunteer force to be raised to support the regular army and by 1861, 200,000 men had joined up. From this movement, the NRA originated to teach these men skills with small arms and to promote rifle shooting as a national pastime. Competition evolved naturally from this and the Prince of Wales became the Association's Patron. Annual meetings were planned and Wimbledon Common was selected as a permanent venue. The first meeting was officially opened by Queen Victoria on 2 July 1860. The Queen fired the first shot from a pre-set rifle using a silken cord attached to the trigger. The main award was the Queen's own prize of £250 which was shot then, as now, from 1000 yards. As London sprawled, so the location became unsuitable for safety reasons and in 1889, the NRA purchased land at Bisley for £12,000 and has been sited there ever since.

A railway was introduced between Brookwood and Bisley in 1890 and the Bisley Bullet steam engine plied between the stations until remarkable celebrations attended the Bullet's last trip in July 1952. During Bisley meetings there were through trains to the ranges from London and extra trains in the Olympic year of 1948.

Walk 4

Distance: *Allow four hours for this walk of six-and-a-half miles*

Turn right from the pub and head for the canal bridge. On the left at the other side of the bridge, join the tow path, remaining on this for a mile-and-a-half through woodland and residential areas until you reach Kiln Bridge, restored in 1981. Tree shaded banks escort you up to Brookwood Lye Bridge where the canal broadens to form a pleasant lake with swans and houseboats. There are more houses on the second section to Kiln Bridge and fast electric trains hum by far up an embankment on your right. Soon the canal bends left, away from the railway and you pass under a footbridge, past Redway Cottages to the urbanisation around Kiln Bridge.

Leave the canal here, cross over the bridge and turn left into Hermitage road at the roundabout. Your target from here is Barrack Path which manifests itself as a road on the far side of the roundabout. Cross with care and proceed along the roadway of Barrack Path until you reach a signal controlled pedestrian crossing. Cross here and presently your path merges with Inkerman Road with school

sausages and onion gravy may tempt you or a Hunters (turkey and veg with a pastry top). A traditional Sunday roast at under £5 is good value. There are many good choices on the menu supplemented by blackboard specials. There is a pleasant garden and good parking where walkers can leave cars (with permission first).
Tel 0483 797240

Fox Inn, Bisley
A painted brick façade on the main road hides a cosy, friendly interior with gas fires and central heating. Alan and Valerie Sparkes have been here for 22 years so there is continuity and contentment. The pub is open 12 hours daily with normal hours on Sunday, and food is available between 12.00-14.30 and 19.00-21.30 each day. It is a Courage house serving their beers and three types of lagers. There is a varied and extensive menu supported by a specials board to suit all tastes. Children are allowed in the restaurant area and there is a large garden and car park (walkers may leave cars if you ask first). Alan and Valerie welcome walkers as they too enjoy walking, when time permits, crossing the road to wander on Bisley Common and Sheets Heath as much as they can. 0483 473175.

playing fields on the left. The Crimean War flavour is maintained as you cross Raglan Road and I am sure you will admire the thirty cottages comprising Wellington Terrace on the right, a relict of the former Inkerman Barracks. You are now on Victoria Road and soon a green appears on your right. At the far end of this, turn right and follow Beechwood Road downhill and through to a junction with Barnby Road where you turn left.

The route hereabouts is rather urban in character but Knaphill is rather a sprawl and I can assure you that greener lands lie ahead. Where Barnby Road meets the Knaphill to Horsell road, turn left and then right into Barley Mow Lane where the parade of shops end. Look out for Waterers Rise on your left and opposite this, enter Waterers Park on the right. Turn left alongside a hedge and then past a brick building, keeping the same alignment to join a well worn path

Bisley Church

entering woodland. Ignore all crossing paths until you emerge into an area of grassland where you immediately turn right keeping the trees on your right. As you approach some small trees ahead take the path which curves left. Ignore all diverging paths and enter a woodland strip of oak and beech, soon reaching Chobham Road. Turn left here then quickly right into Warburg Lane following this narrow lane past Hill Place Farm and looking out for the entrance drive to Bisley Church on the left. Pass through the gateway and up the gravel drive to the church which is dedicated to St. John the Baptist and is a lovely and lonely church. Standing away from the houses of Bisley to the west, it is built of local sandstone with a wooden tower surmounted by a short tiled spire. A fine yew guards the old wooden porch but the door was locked as we passed with no note to indicate where the key could be found. Locked church doors are commonplace these days, a sad reflection on our day and age.

From the yew tree outside the church porch, head directly for a metal kissing gate passing through and following the hedge left-handed until you reach a stile by a metal gate. Cross this and turn right on to the track ahead which you follow until you meet the busy A322 with the inviting Fox Inn to your right if you fancy refreshments. Cross the main road with care to follow the track directly opposite.

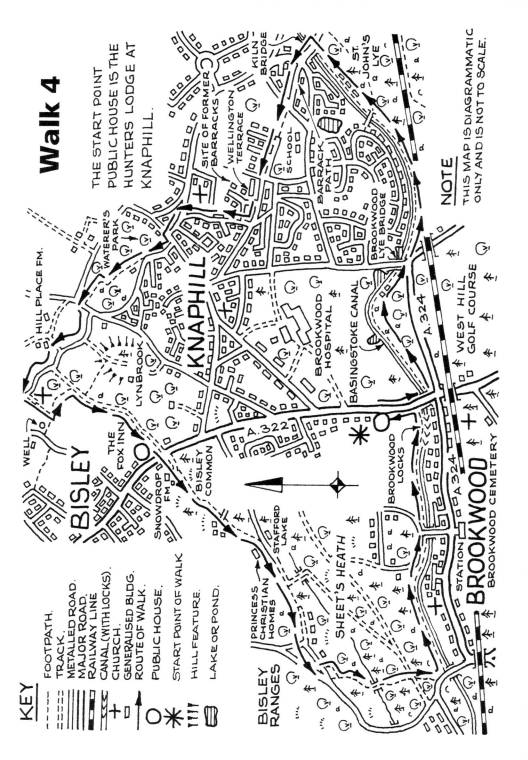

Walk 4

THE START POINT PUBLIC HOUSE IS THE HUNTERS LODGE AT KNAPHILL.

NOTE

THIS MAP IS DIAGRAMMATIC ONLY AND IS NOT TO SCALE.

KEY

--- --- FOOTPATH.
===== TRACK.
||||| METALLED ROAD.
||||| MAJOR ROAD.
RAILWAY LINE
CANAL (WITH LOCKS).
+ CHURCH.
☐ GENERALISED BLDG.
➤ ROUTE OF WALK.
O PUBLIC HOUSE.
✳ START POINT OF WALK
||||| HILL FEATURE.
▨ LAKE OR POND.

BISLEY

BISLEY RANGES

KNAPHILL

BROOKWOOD

BROOKWOOD CEMETERY

HILL PLACE FM.

WATERER'S PARK

THE FOX INN

SNOWDROP FM

BISLEY COMMON

A.322

LYNBROOK

WELL

SITE OF FORMER BARRACKS

WELLINGTON TERRACE

KILN BRIDGE

ST. JOHN'S LYE

SCHOOL

BARRACK PATH

BROOKWOOD LYE BRIDGE

BASINGSTOKE CANAL

BROOKWOOD HOSPITAL

A.324

WEST HILL GOLF COURSE

BROOKWOOD LOCKS

STAFFORD LAKE

SHEET'S HEATH

PRINCESS CHRISTIAN HOMES

STATION

A.324

You now enter Bisley Common and as with all commons, it is criss crossed by paths in all directions, so take care and follow the instructions. The bridleway you are on is marked as No 147 on the metal signpost and you pass through a relatively young woodland of silver birch, oak and hazel. As the track swings right into the nicely named Snowdrop Farm, take the path left of this and straight away fork right alongside a wooden fence. At a marker post, take the left fork and follow a pleasant path through young trees and over two crossing paths before sinking into a narrow gully to proceed across the access to Strawberry Farm on your right. Soon you cross over another path and join a track which swings right as you pass a metal gate with paddocks beyond. As the track forks, keep right over recently laid road scalpings which quickly end and proceed on a muddy track over an access road to join a

Brookwood Lock

metalled road, where you turn right-handed over the bridge with metal balustrades and the date 1900 displayed. You now pass the attractive, clean façade of the Princess Christian Homes administered by the Forces Help Society gifted by Lord Pirbright in 1900.

The road becomes a track which you follow past Hawthorn Cottage to a gate which leads you on to a path into young woodland. Keep right at the fork to follow a winding path, crossing a track to join an access track to properties which appear to the left. Meet a metalled road, turning left to pass right-handed of a barrier. With open common land to your right, approach a similar barrier which appears ahead. Angle left before the barrier and keep parallel with the road across an area of tarmac picking up a path on the far side and continue until another path crosses your own from a nearby roadside lay-by to the right. Turn left and follow the path around a gorsebush soon entering deciduous woodland where a well-defined route leads over a metal railed footbridge. Proceed directly ahead, ignoring side paths, uphill to a small clearing where another path crosses. Continue across the clearing angling slightly right to soon cross a wide track to follow a winding path downhill through woodland and on to a road. Go left-handed down the road to join the Basingstoke Canal by turning left as you reach the bridge. Follow the path back to Brookwood Locks and Brookwood Bridge, then left-handed past the garage back to the Hunters Lodge.

A military lake and rhododendrons from Minley

Background to the Walk

On the fringe of an area which has developed to an unrecognisable extent over the past century, lies a scattered community called Minley with a few cottages, farms, a pub, a manor and a barracks. You may be excused for not noticing it as you pass through on the A327. However, it was mentioned in Domesday as Mindeslei — so it has antiquity, the name probably derived from Mynda's wood or clearing. There are many woods around here interspersed with sandy heathlands, poor land for agriculture.

A pamphlet written in 1387 mentions a manor, so there has been a Minley Manor for over 600 years. The present building dates from 1858 and was designed by Henry Clutton in the style of the French Renaissance, for Raikes Currie a wealthy London banker and radical MP. Royalty have visited the Manor in recent times following the house's purchase for the Royal Engineers in 1971. The Queen, as Colonel-in-Chief of the Royal Engineers, visited in October 1976 when she laid the foundation stone for the new Gibraltar Barracks opposite. This is military country and since Aldershot became the home of the British Army in 1854, the tentacles of the military have eased themselves stealthily into areas either side of the Upper Blackwater valley. You will see evidence of the Royal Engineers during the walk as you pass Hawley Lake.

Minley has a church but it is not a parish in its own right. It was built in 1870 by Raikes Currie in memory of his wife. It is a small church near the Manor, dedicated to St. Andrew, built of flint and sandstone and designed by the same Henry Clutton who master-

Maps
Landranger 1:50,000
Sheet 186
Pathfinder 1:25,000
Sheet 1205 SU85/95
Map Reference of Start/
Finish SU834571

How to get there
From Farnham take A325 northbound to Farnborough where you take the newly classified route A327 left-handed at the roundabout and follow it over the new motorway junction 4A with M3. The Crown and Cushion lies on your left-hand side half a mile north of the junction. From Camberley take A30 westbound through Blackwater turning left on to A327 just past the Ely Hotel. Follow A327 south past the entrance to Gibraltar Barracks on your left for a little over one mile. You will find the Crown and Cushion on your right. The Tillingborne Bus Company service F39 between Yateley and Farnborough passes the Crown and Cushion at Minley. It is a limited service so it would be wise policy to check with the Company on 0252 315900. Alternatively Tillingbourne service F40 which plys between Camberley and Farnham via Fleet, passes the junction of Sandy Lane and Minley Road near Guillemont

Fields, from where it is a half a mile walk north westwards to the Crown and Cushion. The walk could also be joined at Blackwater (Hawley Road, London Road, Frogmore Road roundabout) by using Stagecoach services 25 or 200 from Camberley. If you are travelling from Farnham, service F40 as described above may be the best route either alighting and walking from Guillemont Fields or joining the walk at Hawley Church.

Pub facilities
Crown and Cushion, Minley

This fine, popular pub dating back 400 years lies end on to Minley Road, with a tree shaded patio stretching the full length of the pub itself and the adjacent, recently constructed, Meade Hall. Flower beds, tubs and hanging baskets gave a summer glow to an already attractive pub when I called. The pub's name commemorates the crowning of the last Saxon King, Harold, who lost his life at Hastings. The yew tree standing by the pub was once fashioned by a topiarist to resemble a crown standing on a cushion. Inside is a long bar with beamed ceiling and brick fireplaces. This is the Crown Bar where you can sample home cooked meat and potato pie, steak rolls and onions or a pizza wedge amongst other mouth watering attractions. Satisfy your appetite every day between 12.00-14.30 and 19.00-21.30. The pub is run by Allied (Ind Coope) Breweries and offers Tetleys, Burtons, John Smiths and one guest ale (Marstons Pedigree when I called). Lager lovers can indulge in Castlemaine,

The Crown and Cushion at Minley

minded the architecture of the Manor. It also has a physical link as the church bell was once the fire bell at the Manor.

Not far away to the north, the old Exeter trunk road (A30) cuts straight over Hartford Bridge Flats, a fearsome, desolate heath in the old stage coach days, where, with an anxious look over his shoulder, the coachman would whip up his horses to avoid the highwaymen and footpads who haunted this place. He may have been unlucky enough to encounter Dick Turpin or Parson Darby on the heath, the latter living out his life between the pulpit and the highwayman's mask. His days as a reverend and a villain ended on the gallows. Hundreds of years earlier, King John in sour mood, rode with his entourage along this way in 1215 from his castle at Odiham to Runnymede and the Magna Carta.

There is yet another villain in these parts who lived in the times of a later king. Making sure that he ended up on the winning side in the Civil War, Colonel Thomas Blood gained lands in Ireland which he subsequently lost at the Restoration. Living at Minley Warren, he was involved in numerous criminal acts culminating in the theft of the Royal Regalia from the Tower in 1671 when the Keeper of the jewels was stabbed. Stuffing the gems under his cloak he made off but lost them when his horse stumbled on leaving the Tower.

*Carlsberg and Lowenbrau during the hours of
11.30-23.00 (Mon-Sat) in summer (hours vary
in winter) and the usual hours of 12.00-15.00
and 19.00-22.30 on Sundays. Cold food is
always available during opening times. The
pub's pride and joy is **The Meade Hall**, a
cunning modern construction made up skilfully
from the fabric of two 400-year-old barns, one
from Surrey and one from Wiltshire. It was
opened to the public in March 1980 and would
fool the connoisseur with its authenticity. It is
high roofed, impressive and packed with farm
and other implements. A long, rough-hewn table
occupies central position with side tables along
the walls, a bar and a food counter. There is a
good range of food listed on the blackboard and a
fire roars during winter months in a massive
brick fireplace. It is a very popular pub with a
large car park where walkers can leave their cars
with permission. Tel 0252 545253.*

He escaped but was arrested while
enjoying his ale at the Crown and
Cushion. Brought before Charles II,
the King guffawed with laughter at
Blood's audacity, gave him a pension
and restored his Irish lands. So a criminal was rewarded yet the fate of the
wounded keeper is unrecorded.

The Meade Hall at the Crown and Cushion

We visit Hawley on this walk, now swallowed up by the Blackwater conurbation — but before we condemn its lost identity, I would like to quote Nora Hough
from her book *Our Village — I remember, you remember:*—
Set on the borders of Hampshire / Midst bracken and heather and pine /
Possessing no outstanding feature / No ruins, nor manor house fine / But a
beautiful church where we worship / Facing on to a tree bordered green / A hall,
a school and the river / The cottages dotted between / Whose folk are friendly and
helpful / There are wooded walks, pleasant to roam / Just a typical village of
England / But the place I shall always call home.

Walk 5

Distance: *Allow three hours for this walk of five miles*
Leave the pub and cross over the main road to join a pleasant, tree shaded metalled
pathway on the far side. Turn left and parallel the main road until turning right on
to a track opposite wooden gates. Follow the track through woodland to where it
meets another, turning right at this point to follow the track which gently curves
left. Ignore three separate tracks on the right and after the third one look out for
a left turning track, noting the bridleway marker post on the right indicating your

route. Initially the route is muddy and there is a diversionary path to the left which soon rejoins the main track where it turns sharply right through profuse rhodo-dendrons. Continue ahead until the track veers left to the sandy shore of Hawley Lake. On the lake's far side you will see the military buildings and equipment of the Royal Engineers, whose flag flies proudly from its mast.

A shallow bank of sand rises to your right, a feature which stretches desert like for about 300 yards. Your route follows the left-hand edge of this nearest to the lake. As you cross the burning sand (it was a warm summer's day when I walked the route), you are compensated by the sight of cool waters of island dotted Hawley Lake nearby. The sand belt soon narrows down to a track and you can still glimpse the lake on your left. Swans and light sailing craft enjoyed its placid pine girt waters as I passed. Soon you reach a metalled lane where an inlet of the lake noses into the woodland. Follow the lane left-handed and immediately turn right by a bridleway marker post to pick up a straight bridleway which fringes the northernmost houses of Cove. Turn left and continue through oak, birch and pine woodland to a crossing of tracks where you turn left and soon renew acquaintance with the lane you briefly encountered earlier. Follow the lane straight ahead until you meet another metalled road where you go to the right.

Where the road starts to swing left take a track which angles off right and follow this through pine and birch over two track crossings. The track gradually rises as you approach the low summit of Hawley Hill lying to your left, but not prominent as a topographical feature. Shortly, a track joins obliquely from the left and just past here I was surprised to find a copper beech mixed in with acid soil-loving pines and sweet chestnuts. It seemed quite at ease with its heathland neighbours. Following this, another track joins from the left, while a path leads off right before your main track forks. Take the left-hand fork and descend from Hawley Hill, passing under low voltage transmission lines to follow a pleasant, firm surfaced track down a valley wooded on each side. Shortly after a track joins from the left, you will glimpse a brick house ahead. At this point, look for a woodland path diverging right indicated by a footpath marker post.

Leave the track here and follow the path through dense rhododendrons initially and then to the left of a wire netting fence until you reach a tarmac road. Through a gap in the hedge opposite you will see the Victorian parish church of Hawley across the well trimmed green. As it is usually locked it is best to continue your walk by turning left and passing through two sets of metal barriers to an access road which shortly meets Hawley Road.

Turn left by East Lodge and continue along Hawley Road up to the roundabout where you pass to the left, crossing the twin carriageways of Woodside to find a bridleway sign on your left which you join by passing between low concrete posts. Follow the path until you meet a metalled lane and continue on this uphill. This is a military road and the speed limit for vehicles is 15 mph. While it is very quiet, there are parallel paths which you can use, the first being across the corner of a right-hand bend and the second, a long one, which parallels the lane as it passes

Walk 5

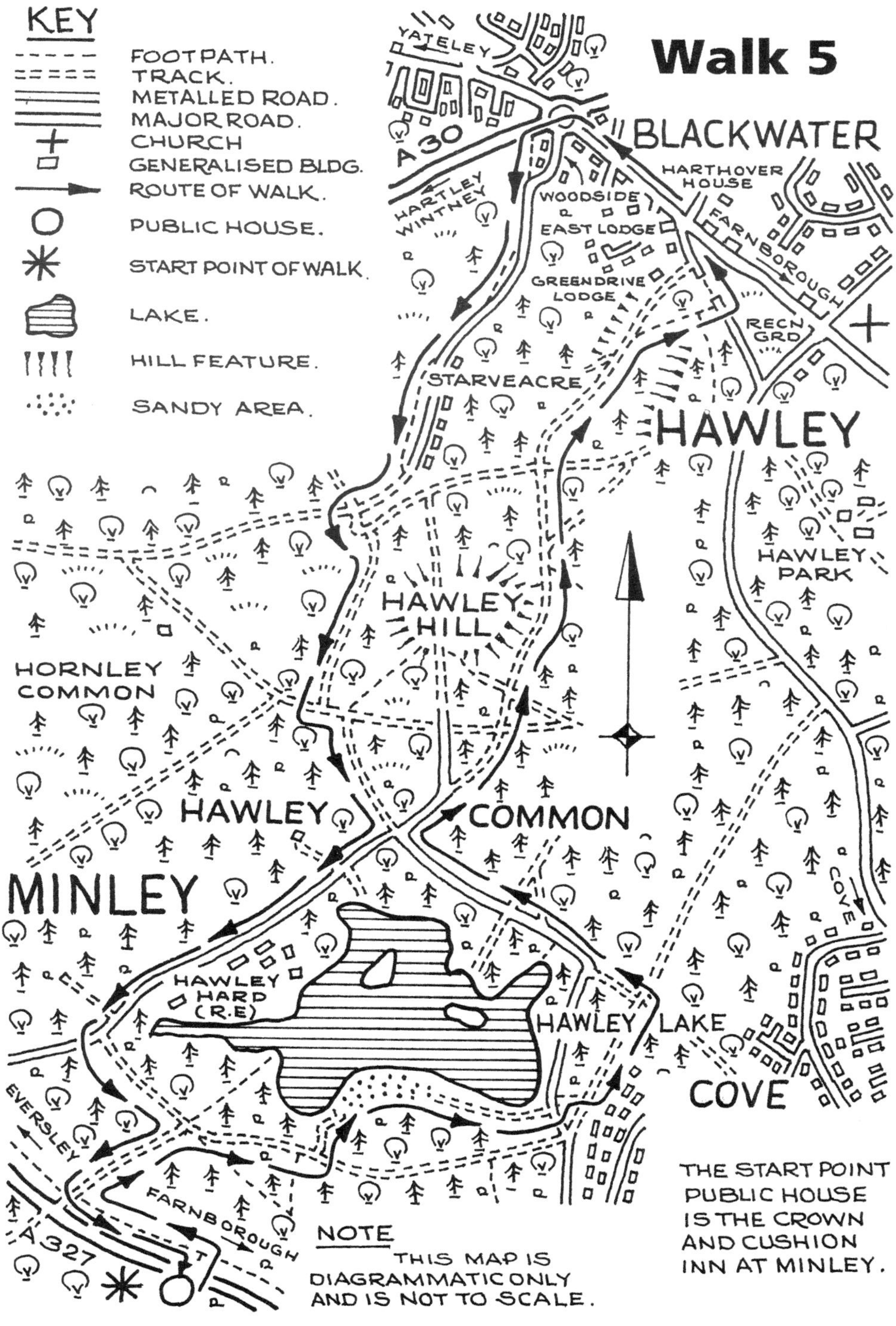
KEY
FOOTPATH.
TRACK.
METALLED ROAD.
MAJOR ROAD.
CHURCH
GENERALISED BLDG.
ROUTE OF WALK.
PUBLIC HOUSE.
START POINT OF WALK.
LAKE.
HILL FEATURE.
SANDY AREA.
YATELEY
A 30
BLACKWATER
HARTLEY WINTNEY
WOODSIDE
EAST LODGE
GREENDRIVE LODGE
HARTHOVER HOUSE
FARNBOROUGH
RECN GRD
STARVEACRE
HAWLEY
HAWLEY PARK
HAWLEY HILL
HORNLEY COMMON
HAWLEY COMMON
MINLEY
HAWLEY HARD (R.E)
HAWLEY LAKE
COVE
COVE
EVERSLEY
FARNBOROUGH
A 327
NOTE
THIS MAP IS DIAGRAMMATIC ONLY AND IS NOT TO SCALE.
THE START POINT PUBLIC HOUSE IS THE CROWN AND CUSHION INN AT MINLEY.

Hawley Church

a line of houses called Starve Acre. The lane passes through a wooden gate and continues through pines and eventually swings left as two tracks veer off to the right. A solitary silver birch stands as a sentinel with a bridleway marker post beneath it. As the lane turns even further left, take a track leading right indicated by a marker post.

A pleasant trackway now takes you southwards between silver birch and pines straight to a T junction of tracks where you turn left and almost immediately right on to a track which is at first sandy and then muddy, but the muddy patch may be avoided by taking a well trodden path to the left. The track soon reaches a crossroads which you may recognise from the outward journey. Turn right to follow a metalled road alongside Hawley Lake and past the Royal Engineers Depot at Hawley Hard, guarded by a high wire mesh fence. There are occasional road humps as you follow the wide road around a left-hand bend and past a high metal gate on your right bearing a terse Keep Out message. Where the road bends right, take the track leading off to your left passing to the left of a wooden gate and continuing through woodland to where another track joins from the right. Turn right and follow this, recognising that this is the track you used in the initial part of your outward journey. Turn left at the wooden gate and follow the metalled path back to the Crown and Cushion.

Sandy hills and deep green waters from Frimley Green

Background to the Walk

The area known as Frimley Green has not always enjoyed that name, as formerly the scattering of cottages and farms was known less attractively as Frimley South End. Not that farms in the Blackwater Valley thrived, as the poverty of the soil then was as great as it is now. However, a fair quantity of grain stuffs were grown in the district as the old windmill off Guildford Road proves. The tower has now been incorporated into a modern structure.

The Frimley part of the name derives from 'Fremma' (a saxon name) and 'Leah' (a woodland or clearing) and the present spelling has been used since 1575. Frimley Green lies on the eastern fringes of the built up area comprising Aldershot and Farnborough astride the A321 as it wends its urban way between Ash and Camberley. However, to the east, military lands stretch their pine and heather clad wastes over to Pirbright and Brookwood. Highwaymen, in days gone by, made good use of these wastes with the Golden Farmer and Claude Duval surprising hapless travellers on the heaths. The latter was a chivalrous man, polite and charming to the ladies but relieving them of their money and jewellery all the same. His home was a thatched cottage on the Frimley Ridges. Less menacing were the sheep driven along the ancient Maultway which led along the nearby Chobham Ridges from the Hampshire Downs towards London. The name derives from the Celtic 'Mollt' which means sheep. There are Celtic barrows on the Ridges.

Frimley failed to get a mention in the Domesday as it was part of the manor of Henley at Pirbright. It was

Maps
Landranger 1:50,000
Sheet 186
Pathfinder 1:25,000
Sheet 1205 SU85/95
Map Reference of Start/
Finish SU891564

How to get there
From the large roundabout to the east of Farnham, take the exit signed A324. Follow this through Badshot Lea and then join A323 eastbound towards Guildford, taking A321 (signed Frimley) left-handed at the roundabout through Ash Vale and Mytchett to Frimley Green. Turn right at the double mini roundabout on B3012, soon crossing the railway to find the Kings Head on your left. From Camberley take A321 southbound to the double mini roundabout at Frimley Green where you turn left to join B3012. After crossing the railway you will find the Kings Head on your left. There are many bus services between Farnham and Aldershot including Stagecoach services 219 and 268. From Aldershot Bus Station, Stagecoach regular service 550 takes you to Frimley Green (Rose and Thistle) where you alight and follow Guildford Road (B3012) for a short walk to the

*Kings Head. From Camberley,
the same Stagecoach service
550 leaves Camberley Station.
Alight at Frimley Green and
follow Guildford Road
(B3012) to the Kings Head*

Pub facilities
Kings Head,
Frimley Green

*Sandwiched between railway
and canal, the pub presents an
attractive picture with its
cream-painted brickwork
contrasting with the modern
brickwork of the right-hand
side extension. On the other
side is a spacious garden with
swings, slide and a crazy
house together with many
picnic tables. This is a
Harvester free house and has a
popularity in the area.
Opening hours are from
11.00-15.00 and 17.00-23.00
(Mon-Fri), 11.00-23.00 (Sat)
and normal Sunday opening
times of 12.00-15.00 and
19.00-22.30. During these
hours you can enjoy John
Smiths, Courage Best and
Bass. There are others in
winter which you can sample
in the Victorian style three-
sided bar with brown and
cream decorations and
carpeted throughout. Fosters
and Kronenberg lagers are on
offer together with Beamish
Stout and Dry Blackthorn
Cider. The Harvester menu is
supported by a specials board
which you can order from
either in the restaurant or the
bar. There is more than
enough to suit all tastes
including an extensive
vegetarian choice and a good
children's menu. There is a
good range of basket meals
together with char grills and
bakehouse plaits followed by a
tempting dessert menu. Sit
down and enjoy your meal*

The Kings Head at Frimley Green

also part of the Royal hunting forest of Windsor which was, in former times, divided into 'bailiwicks' and 'walkes'. Frimley Walke lay in the bailiwick of Bagshot under the jurisdiction of a park keeper. Much wooded land still remains, particularly to the east of A321. Frimley Lodge Park, lying between Frimley Green and Mytchett is 61 acres in extent, managed by the local Borough Council of Surrey Heath. The park, formerly grazing land and deciduous wood, was opened to the public in 1987 and borders the Basingstoke canal. Local people find a great range of facilities here.

The development of Frimley Green in the 19th Century was rapid, mainly due to three factors. First was the coming of the Nine Elms (London) — Southampton railway in 1838-1840 which provided an outlet and attracted people from London to a handily placed, healthy, pine-clad countryside. Before this, the Basingstoke Canal arrived in 1796 bringing trade from London and the Thames via the River Wey up to New Haw where the canal's eastern terminus was built. Built by Irish navvies, the canal cuts straight through high ground at Deepcut via a series of locks and enters the Blackwater Valley at Frimley Green where it turns up to Ash, crosses the river by an aqueduct and heads west towards Fleet and Basingstoke. The third factor was the numerous military establishments which mushroomed in the area from 1854 bringing personnel and *between 12.00-14.30 and 17.30-22.30 (Mon-Fri), all day on Saturday and 12.00-14.30 and 19.00-22.00 on Sunday (although the restaurant is open all day). The Kings Head was built in the 1930s and has always been a pub, although it was not until March 1991 that Harvester took the pub over. Children are allowed in all parts of the pub and walkers are welcome to leave their cars in the ample car park after asking permission first. Tel 0252 835431.*

Right: The Basingstoke Canal Centre at Mytchett

trade to the area. There is however another more recent factor. Having had invasions by the canal and railway followed by the Army, Frimley now has the M3 motorway which has made commuting and trade to the London area a great deal easier since opening in 1972.

A tragic figure passed through Frimley Green on 21 December 1648. A large body of heavily armed, mounted troopers made their way through the area on a damp and gloomy day, escorting a dignified, stubborn enemy of Cromwell's Commonwealth. He was Charles I on his way from his period of incarceration at Carisbrooke Castle on the Isle of Wight, to his trial and execution in London in January 1649. The prisoner and his escort spent the night at the home of Lord and Lady Newburgh, ostensibly tenants of the deposed King at the Royal Lodge at Bagshot. While on the morbid subject of executions, the last men to be publicly executed at Frimley Green were three men hung for the murder of the parish priest at the Parsonage in 1850. Naturally the Parsonage was said to be haunted for years afterwards.

In the past there has been trouble between the canal and the railway at Frimley Green where a fine, solid-looking aqueduct takes the former over the latter. The structure sprung a leak and this trickle of water once caused the railway to be closed. The escaping water damped the fires of steam locomotives passing beneath and caused their fires to go out.

Walk 6

Distance: *Allow three hours for this five mile walk*

Emerging from the Kings Head, veer left and cross the road, taking an unsigned path diverging right just past the Frimley Lodge entrance. This leads you to the Basingstoke Canal towing path which you follow right-handed past the extensive pleasure and recreation grounds of Frimley Lodge Park. At weekends, this section of the canal path is popular, due to the access from the park and the Basingstoke Canal Centre on the left further down at Mytchett. Many craft and pleasure boats cluster around the Centre.

At the bridge just below the Centre, reluctantly leave the canal, turning left to cross the weight restricted bridge and on your right you will see the modern Potters Steak House which has undoubtedly benefited from the restoration of the 200-year-old waterway. Almost opposite to the Steak House entrance, a track goes left towards a metal gate. Do not go through the gate but turn right through a barrier and follow a straight track gently uphill through oak, birch and ash. Ignore all side tracks and reach the top of a steep section by taking the left-hand of three parallel tracks.

Over the summit on heathland, you will find that the main track soon swings left. At this point, take a lesser-used track which angles right and you will find that surrounding vegetation soon closes in as you thread your way downhill to meet a multiple track junction. Ignore the two tracks immediately to your left and look ahead to where two tracks fork in front of you in a clear area backed by pines. Take the left-hand fork which curves gently left.

The problem with these Surrey heaths and commons is that they are a maze of tracks and paths so these follow instructions carefully. Ignore any side tracks and proceed to meet a track from the right, noting a pine topped conical hill in front of you and an open hill in the distance on the right. Turn left here on to the main track and head towards yet more track junctions. Here the route lies directly ahead up a sharp rise in the heathland and as you labour up this, ignore all side tracks. At the summit, your path swings right and then left. Two lesser tracks diverge right before you plunge into and out of a shallow depression and soon curve around to the right as tracks join from the left.

As you curve right, note a flat area over to your left behind a bank which appears to serve as a car park and directly after this the track forks. Take the left-hand track which appears to go back on itself after being joined by a link track from the right and then as it turns further left towards the car park mentioned above, take a faint track straight ahead which soon becomes a path leading over a ditch, across a track and over another ditch on the far side. Directions become a little easier now as you enter an expansive area of clear ground which rather looks as though it has been devastated by fire in recent years. There is a slightly charred look about this treeless waste. Follow the path to the crest of a hill. It is an ill wind which blows no one any good, because the lack of trees gives superb views northwards over the pinelands of West Surrey towards Camberley and Windsor Forest.

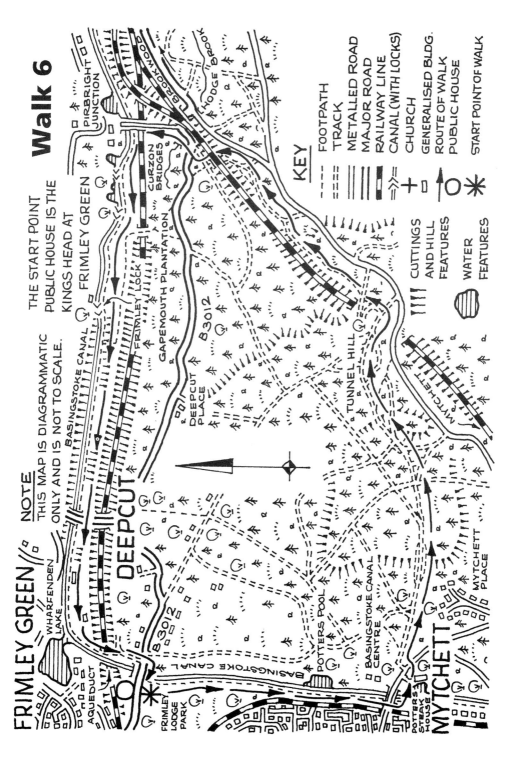

Walk 6

FRIMLEY GREEN

THE START POINT PUBLIC HOUSE IS THE KINGS HEAD AT FRIMLEY GREEN

NOTE
THIS MAP IS DIAGRAMMATIC ONLY AND IS NOT TO SCALE.

KEY

- - - - FOOTPATH
- - - - TRACK
||||| METALLED ROAD
||||| MAJOR ROAD
||||| RAILWAY LINE
=〉=〉= CANAL (WITH LOCKS)
+ CHURCH
□ GENERALISED BLDG.
○ PUBLIC HOUSE
✳ START POINT OF WALK

↑↑↑↑ CUTTINGS AND HILL FEATURES

WATER FEATURES

PIRBRIGHT JUNCTION

HODGE BROOK

CURZON BRIDGES

FRIMLEY LOCK

GAPEMOUTH PLANTATION

B3012

DEEPCUT PLACE

TUNNEL HILL

MYTCHETT

BASINGSTOKE CANAL

WHARFENDEN LAKE

AQUEDUCT

B3012

DEEPCUT

FRIMLEY LODGE PARK

POTTERS POOL

BASINGSTOKE CANAL CENTRE

MYTCHETT PLACE

POTTERS STEAK HOUSE

MYTCHETT

From these breezy heights your path twists down dramatically and then rises a little to ease round the shoulder of a hill. To your left, you may have caught glimpses of the Aldershot to Woking railway, deep in its cutting before it plunges under Tunnel Hill over which you recently crossed. The railway tunnel is 418 yards long and the line was opened on 2 May 1870. Your path has now blossomed out into a track and passes high above the railway, before veering right to drop into a valley still in open, sandy, heathland country. In the valley bottom, turn left at a track junction and rise again only to descend with a line of pines on your left. You shortly arrive at a spot where rain has gouged out steep gullies in the yielding sand. Two ways present

The path at Longdown Hill

themselves here, but your best route is right-handed where you drop to the valley bottom, turning left on a low level track. Keep straight ahead, ignoring side tracks until you turn left and pass under the railway by a single arched brick bridge. Turn right at the track crossing ahead and make your way down to the Frimley to Woking road passing to the left of a rusty gate. Go right on the road, crossing over Hodge Brook and where it bends right to pass under the railway, go straight ahead to the left of a barrier with an old concrete pill box away on your left. The metalled road you now follow uphill, has seen happier days as centre line marking is still evident. Cross over the Waterloo — Southampton railway line and then turn right down on to the Basingstoke Canal tow path, following this left under the bridge.

So now you are back on the canal and I am sure you will admire the quiet sylvan beauty of this part. Still, green waters reflect the greenery above as you pass along the bank and fishermen fervently hope for a catch. Water trickles and splashes through closed lock gates. This sets the scene for the next mile and a half but I will not describe it further, leaving you to sample its serenity. Look out for an oak tree seemingly growing out of the water, a rough hewn canal side chair made out of a tree trunk, willow trees on a little island and a lock Keeper's cottage. Pass under Deepcut Bridge, built in 1938 and refurbished in 1990. Garden gnomes will watch you from the far side and a pipeline crosses the waterway before the canal eventually bends sharply right and crosses the railway by way of an aqueduct. After this you join an access road which drifts further away from the canal. When you meet a road turn right, cross the bridge and back to the Kings Head.

Military and pastoral lands from Pirbright

WALK 7
Allow 1 ¹/₂ hours
2 ¹/₂ miles
Walk begins page 43

Background to the Walk

The village of Pirbright is sandwiched between the extensive military lands comprising Pirbright Common on the west and to the east, the 400 acres of Brookwood Cemetery. The pride of the village is its fine green and its tranquil duck pond, well-loved and treasured by the villagers. The derivation of the name Pirbright came from 'sparse woodland where pear trees grow'. There is plenty of woodland here though as this area once was a part of the Royal hunting forest of Windsor, the village being within its boundaries up to 1694. The main road between Woking and Aldershot disturbs the peace of the village, but to the west we find a serene enclave around the parish church of St. Michael and All Angels, which has been a place of worship for at least 800 years. We pass the battlemented tower with its small oak shingled spire on the walk and it is worth pausing to glance inside.

The present church stands on the site of an older one which had become so dilapidated in the reign of George III that a brief was issued to rebuild it, the resultant cost estimate being £2000. It may be a surprise that durable stone can be excavated in this area by digging down less than one metre on the surrounding sandy commons. The stone for the tower was quarried nearby but the supply of local stone came to a halt when the Army took over 3,000 acres of Pirbright Common in the 1870s. Inside the church, a fine gallery extended over the west end of the nave and later over the north aisle too. An orchestra of wind and string instruments accompanied the choir who sat in the west gallery and it was only in 1973 that the north gallery was removed.

Maps
Landranger 1:50,000
Sheet 186
Pathfinder 1:25,000
Sheet 1205 SU85/95
Map Reference of Start/
Finish SU945543

How to get there
From the large roundabout east of Farnham take A324 to Ash where you temporarily join A323 towards Guildford, resuming A324 to the left shortly afterwards. The Royal Oak lies on your right before you reach Pirbright and just before the B380 turn off to Woking. From Camberley take A321 to Frimley Green where you fork left on to B3012. About half a mile after passing under the railway bridge take B3405 straight ahead to join A324 where you turn right passing through Pirbright village. Keep right south of the village where B3032 goes on towards Guildford. The Royal Oak lies to your left just after passing the B380 turn off to Woking. There are no regular bus services past the Royal Oak but you can join the walk east of Causeway Farm by alighting from the Guildford and West Surrey service 554 at the west end of Connaught Road Brookwood by the railway arch. Walk through

the arch, cross over B3012 which turns right and look for a footpath on the opposite side which leads across to School Lane (B3405) where you can join the walk. The 554 regular service (Farnborough - Woking) operates hourly (not Sundays). From Camberley you can join this route by way of Stagecoach services 549 and 550, alighting at the Rose and Thistle Frimley Green. From Farnham take one of the many services to Aldershot Bus Station and change to Stagecoach Service 549 or 550 alighting at the Rose and Thistle at Frimley Green to pick up service 554 to Brookwood.

Pub facilities
Royal Oak,
Pirbright

To the traveller passing by on the curving A324, the pub comes into view with a certain splendour which, having passed, may prompt many to turn round and come back. This gabled half tiled pub with whitewashed brickwork at lower levels stands amid pleasant, well tended gardens with picnic benches on the paved area next to the stream. Wooden two rail ranch fencing completes the immaculate scene. Inside the pub is full of beams and atmosphere, there are nooks and crannies everywhere with chairs and settles and even some old church pews. An inglenook fireplace with a copper hood provides cheer in the winter. You can sample the delights of this 150 year old pub from 11.00-23.00 six days a week with the usual hours of 12.00-15.00 and 19.00-22.30 (on Sunday) The Royal Oak is a Wayside Inn

The Royal Oak at Pirbright

In the churchyard you will find a granite monolith said to weigh 6 tons which was hauled here with difficulty from Dartmoor. This commemorates Henry Morton Stanley, African explorer, finder of Dr. David Livingstone, and one-time resident of the parish. In spite of the fame of his exploits, he was denied burial in Westminster Abbey with Livingstone and lies here in a quiet Surrey churchyard. His final years were spent at Furze Hill, north west of the village, where he perpetuated his African adventures by creating fantasy names in the area such as Congo Stream, Ruwenzori Hill and Mazamboni Farm.

On the walk you will follow the perimeter of Pirbright Common where red flags fly when there is firing on the ranges. The Commonlands, called the 'waste lands' of Pirbright Manor, were sold to the Army in the 1870s as a training ground for the Brigade of Guards. Their existing camp over towards Mytchett consisted of canvas tents on concrete bases, but gradually permanent barracks replaced this flimsy housing. As you walk, you will see heathland stretching far to the west in a sea of pine, bracken and heather — a fine habitat for wild life. The village of Pirbright may indeed feel thankful that the Army has prevented the spread of Aldershot and Farnborough this far east by their purchase of the Common.

On the other side of Pirbright lies the vast pine-clad Brookwood Cemetery, advertised as a burial ground 'midst Surrey pines'. In 1850 the cemeteries of London were becoming overcrowded and several had reached the point were no more burials were possible. In an attempt to solve this problem, the London Necropolis and Mausoleum Company purchased 2,268 acres of what was then Woking Common. Fortunately for the living in these parts, only 400 acres were ultimately used for the dead. The cemetery was opened and consecrated on 7 November 1854 for all religious denominations. A three-quarter mile branch railway line was built from the main line at Brookwood and a daily train from a London terminus, alongside Waterloo Bridge Road, ran to the cemetery with special hearse carriages attached. When the terminus at Waterloo Station was partly destroyed by enemy bombing in 1941, the trains ceased and the track was finally removed from the cemetery in 1953.

Walk 7

Distance: *Allow three hours for this walk of five miles*

Leaving the Royal Oak behind, turn left and cross the main road. To the left of the entrance to Stream Farm Boarding Kennels and Cattery a bridleway sign points down an inviting shaded path. There is also a Ministry of Defence sign which reminds us that the military presence is quite dominant here. Follow the path through pines, birch and gorse, passing a house called Smallbourne on your right to join a metalled access road. Soon you pass through a gate to join another road, turning left to cross the insipid looking Stanford Brook. On your right you will see a footpath sign and a stile leading to a path through dark pines. Continue ahead through trimmed rhododendrons until you see a ditch and a concrete footbridge to your right. Cross the bridge and look across the lily strewn expanse of Henleypark Lake, now used by Army personnel for fishing. Acid-loving plants and trees such as pine, birch, gorse and rhododendron crowd around the water's edge.

The crack of small arms fire rattled over the lake from the nearby ranges but failed to disturb a female mallard and eight chicks making arrows on the still waters. From the footbridge proceed along the lake's eastern margin eventually turning your back on the water to cross a stream and a metalled access road preceded by a metal barrier. Continue forward to reach a second barrier but take the left-hand path immediately before this and follow a pleasant path through

and there are two or three special ales available which constantly change. When we called, Badger Best Bitter, Marstons Pedigree and Abbot Ale were on offer in addition to Stella Artois and Heineken lagers. On the food side of the business, there are two printed menus, one for lunch and one for evening. Additionally there are also blackboard specials. The lunch menu offers six types of sandwiches, four types of ploughmans, five types of jacket potato fillings, 6 types of huffers (brown or white baps with fillings) and several main meals ranging from home made steak and ale pie, lemon sole fillet to vegetable curry. When we called, a new menu was being planned which will feature more home made pies. All this is available between 12.00-14.00, and 19.00-21.00 seven days a week with ploughmans available in the afternoon and tea or coffee all day. There is a small dining room comprising six tables but there are plans for this to be extended. The car park is large and walkers can leave their cars after first asking permission.
Tel 0483 232466.

pines, birch, bracken and scattered oaks until you reach a track and turn right. The reed infested Peatmoor Pond lies to your left on the other side of a wire fence where there are signs warning of dangers when the red flag is flying. It was flying in the distance as we walked up the gravel track curving gently uphill. As your route swings right, a fine vista of a straight undulating track opens up with a dominant red flag flying from a pole atop Chair Hill in the distance. Don't let the red flags worry you — you are safe enough on this side of the fence.

Heathland and pines command the view as your track swings right under Chair Hill and other tracks join from the left. Keep straight ahead to reach a metal gate, passing this and swinging left-handed as a track joins from the right. Take care here as two more tracks join from the right and a path enters trees to your left. You route is the widest track curving right-handed up hill with a parallel track on the left.

Pirbright Church — burial place of Henry Morton Stanley

Shortly these two unite and a wide track takes you down past houses on your left called Long Houses. More deciduous trees flourish here, indicating that the acid soils are being left behind. A little way beyond Long Houses, a track joins from the left by a bridleway sign. Turn hard left here ignoring a parallel track to the left and seek out a right turning signed footpath. Proceed steeply uphill through young conifers and enter a meadow via a stile. Go over the meadow to another stile on the far side and from the top of Hazelacre Hill pass through gorse, hawthorn and oaks down over the meadow to a further stile where your path veers left in woodland and then right over a footbridge. Continue to a lane under oak and holly and a ground cover of stitchwort, cow parsley, bluebells and buttercups. Nature was at its best for us on this Spring day. Turn left on the lane passing Box Cottage, looking attractive with its latticed windows and tiled gables.

Very soon a footpath sign points right over a small stream to join a metalled road leading to Thompsons Close on your right. Ignore this and follow a track straight ahead alongside cottages swinging right and eventually reaching B3405 opposite Causeway Farm. Turn right and walk along the footway past houses until you see a holly-lined footpath on your right opposite a school sign, just past Cooks Green

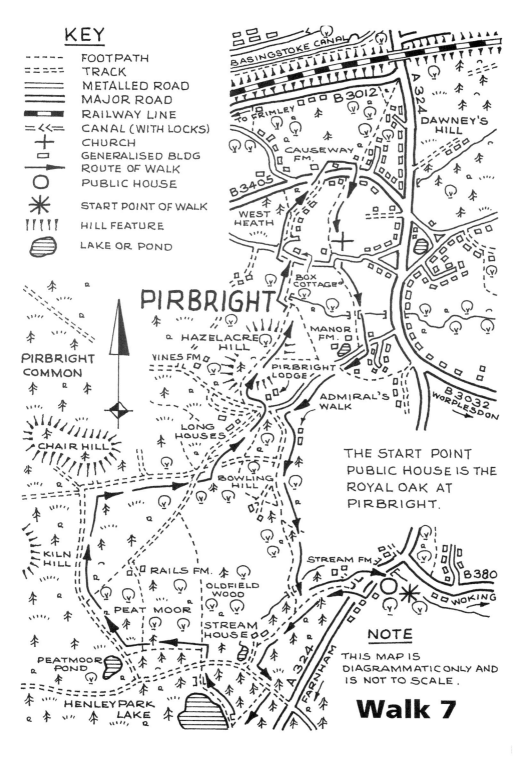

KEY

- `- - - - -` FOOTPATH
- `= = = = =` TRACK
- METALLED ROAD
- MAJOR ROAD
- RAILWAY LINE
- `=<<=` CANAL (WITH LOCKS)
- CHURCH
- GENERALISED BLDG
- ROUTE OF WALK
- PUBLIC HOUSE
- START POINT OF WALK
- HILL FEATURE
- LAKE OR POND

BASINGSTOKE CANAL

A 324

B 3012

TO FRIMLEY

DAWNEY'S HILL

CAUSEWAY FM.

B 3405

WEST HEATH

BOX COTTAGE

PIRBRIGHT

HAZELACRE HILL

MANOR FM.

PIRBRIGHT COMMON

VINES FM.

PIRBRIGHT LODGE

B 3032 WORPLESDON

ADMIRAL'S WALK

CHAIR HILL

LONG HOUSES

BOWLING HILL

THE START POINT PUBLIC HOUSE IS THE ROYAL OAK AT PIRBRIGHT.

KILN HILL

RAILS FM.

OLDFIELD WOOD

STREAM FM.

B 380

WOKING

PEAT MOOR

STREAM HOUSE

A 324

FARNHAM

NOTE

THIS MAP IS DIAGRAMMATIC ONLY AND IS NOT TO SCALE.

PEATMOOR POND

HENLEY PARK LAKE

Walk 7

Cottage. Follow this delightful fenced path to Pirbright Church, pausing to have a peep inside and find Stanley's grave in the churchyard. Join the lane outside the church and follow it right-handed round a left-hand bend. Where it soon bends right, look for a stile in the corner on your left. Cross this and follow a well trodden path with a wire fence on your left until you reach another lane where you bear right. The Old Manor House, still with the remains of a moat, lies on your right, with the Mill House further along, a peaceful part of the old village of Pirbright. On the roadside further along is the sad sight of a dilapidated wooden seat in memory of Geoffrey Arthur Glanville Smith. He was 27 years old when he died in an accident and once lived at Pirbright Lodge opposite. The original name for the house was Mount Byron, built in 1774 by Vice Admiral John Byron, grandfather of the poet. He was dubbed 'Foul weather Jack' because of his ill luck with weather at sea.

The path to Chair Hill

As the metalling ends at Pirbright Lodge, take a track going left with a footpath sign and a chevron sign indicating Admiral's Walk. This is actually the name of a large house you will see on your left, but the track you are on was a favourite walk of John Byron. Descend steeply through woodland forking left where the track divides, soon becoming a woodland path as you pass a gate. Look out for an MOD sign and veer right at a path junction. Rhododendrons press in before you pass a large oak and there are boggy patches before you reach a footbridge and cross a stile into a meadow. With a wire fence on your right follow a well defined path to another stile where you enter mixed woodland. Follow the path through another wet area, over a large diameter concrete culvert pipe to a stile by a gate. Go forward and shortly meet a track that you will recognise from the walk's early stages. Turn left and return to the Royal Oak.

Parklands and waterside ways from Winchfield

WALK 8
Up to 3 hours
5 miles
Walk begins page 50

Background to the Walk

To the railway traveller, Winchfield is a country station with little else in evidence except the Beauclerk Arms pub. When the line from London to Basingstoke was opened in 1839, the village of Winchfield lay about one mile to the south and consisted of a scattered community near the Norman Church of St. Marys. The station was originally known as Shapley Heath, a name which still exists in the locality. Nowadays, the Ordnance Survey places the village name of Winchfield in a position that implies the centre of the village to be at or near the railway station. The name Winchfield means 'open land by a nook or corner' and there is much open agricultural land in this area.

There are four parallel railway tracks passing through the station, two fast and two slow lines. Only slow trains call at Winchfield, the fast trains thundering through at speeds of up to 100 mph on the long straight from east of Basingstoke station to the curve at Farnborough. The Beauclerk Arms was originally called the Railway Tavern in 1842 but was renamed in later years after the Beauclerk family who had built nearby Winchfield House in the 18th Century. There are various family monuments in St. Marys Church, the family being descendants of the first Duke of St. Albans — the natural son of Charles II and Nell Gwynne.

Although Winchfield House lies well outside the scope of this walk, its neighbour, Dogmersfield House lies right on our path and you will pass through its great park with a good view of the house atop its hillock. It is a large Georgian mansion of red brick built in 1728 and is now the home of AMDAHL Interna-

Maps
Landranger 1:50,000
Sheet 186
Pathfinder 1:25,000
Sheet 1204 SU65/75
Map Reference of Start/
Finish SU778538

How to get there
From Farnham take A287 up Castle Street towards Odiham and look out for the B3013 turn off to Fleet on the right after nearly two miles. Take the 4th right turn after passing this junction signed Crookham Village. At the village centre go left again into Dogmersfield where you keep straight on for Winchfield. Look out for the Barley Mow on your right at a cross roads. From Camberley follow A30 Westbound to Hartley Wintney turning left beyond the village to join B3016 at Phoenix Green. Directly after passing under the M3 motorway turn left past Winchfield Station to follow the lane to a cross roads where you swing right. The Barley Mow is on your left at the next cross roads. There is no bus service which passes the Barley Mow but restricted service 208 (Oakley Coaches) serves Dogmersfield en route between Farnham and Odiham. From there it is a three-quarter mile walk along

the lane to the Barley Mow. It would be wise to check with the Company on 0256 780731 first. From Camberley the best route would be to take Hampshire Bus regular service No 200 (Camberley - Basingstoke) and alight either at Winchfield Station (just over a mile's walk to the Barley Mow) or the A287 roundabout east of Odiham taking Broad Oak Lane opposite and join the walk at Broad Oak canal bridge less than half a mile ahead. By British Rail, alight at Winchfield Station and walk from there.

Pub facilities
Barley Mow,
Winchfield

The white-fronted Barley Mow pub sits conspicuously at a cross roads looking over towards the Basingstoke Canal at Barley Mow bridge. It was recently featured in a national advertising campaign and obviously fits the bill as the ad. man's archetypal 'English pub by a village green'. It is a friendly inn with a distinct flavour of cricket to be found inside. A side entrance leads you into the Short Room which is the Barley Mow's answer to the Long Room at Lords. The Short Room is very small indeed, but packed with photographs of the pub's cricket team. Up to two years ago, this was a Courage house and when we visited, the cockerel logo was still perched in prime position. It is now an Ushers house selling Ushers Founders and Ushers Best ales. Courage Best bitter is still on tap and you can enjoy Kronenberg, Hofmeister and Fosters lagers if your fancy

The Barley Mow at Winchfield

tional Management Services Ltd., whose headquarters are in Sunnyvale, California. They are a computing firm who introduced their first processor in 1975.

The house has a slightly longer history as it stands on the site of a palace once owned by the Bishop of Bath and Wells. That wretched monarch Henry VI often stayed there during his long reign and later a love match was hatched within its walls between Prince Arthur, first son of Henry VII, and Catherine of Aragon, who at the tender age of 15, became Arthur's wife. Unfortunately the marriage was brief as Arthur died the following year. We all know what happened to Catherine after that — she married another Tudor, Arthur's brother Henry and so became the first of his six wives. After the Dissolution in the reign of Henry VIII, the house was held by Thomas Wriothesley, First Earl of Southampton and Henry's Chancellor.

Much more interesting was the occupancy of Sir Henry Mildmay in the early 19th Century, who left an indelible mark on the house and its surroundings. He considered that the house was not big enough, so he had it enlarged. He thought the village of Dogmersfield was too close to the house, so he had it moved in 1802 with the church following it into exile during 1806. He considered that Tundry Pond was not big enough so he had it enlarged to twenty acres. He was dissatisfied with Dogmersfield Park, so he set to and had it landscaped to his own satisfaction. Prior to all this, the Basingstoke Canal Company approached him to allow

Broad Oak Bridge on the Basingstoke Canal

the canal to cross his land. Sir Henry flatly refused, so the canal had to trundle around the perimeter.

If you look at a map you can see the loop that the canal had to take to avoid the park. Despite this however, by 1796 the canal was completed from the River Wey at New Haw to Basingstoke, a distance of thirty-seven-and-a-half tortuous miles, especially the Hampshire reaches. The coming of the railway in 1839 led to a decline in the use of the waterway, resulting in the Canal Company being finally wound up in 1869 and the canal sold for £12,000 in 1874. Disuse and decay followed before £50,000 was raised to restore and deepen the canal for the transportation of bricks from works at Up Nately. Unfortunately the clay ran out in 1905 and commercial usage ceased west of Aldershot. Between 1935 and 1973, when restoration work began, the canal died and fell into a neglected state. Restoration work actually began on the stretch of canal you will follow in this walk between the Barley Mow and Broad Oak bridges. The very first stage in the lengthy restoration process was to clear the tow path between these two bridges.

takes you. The pub is popular, with two good sized bars and a pleasant garden with vine covered patio to attract you. In fine summer weather, barbecues are held in the colourful garden. When we called, the landlord was very busy watering, trimming and tending in preparation for the Ushers best pub garden competition. Regulars, visitors and walkers mix happily during opening hours which are 11.00-14.30 and 18.00-23.00 (Mon-Fri), 11.00-15.00, and 18.00-23.00 (Sat) and the usual Sunday times of 12.00-15.00 and 19.00-22.30. A chef looks after the food side of the business and she tempts you by way of a menu and a specials board. Home cooking is the order of the day and the choice is extensive, from omelettes, pastas and home cooked Wiltshire ham to Suffolk hot pot and gammon, leek and mushroom risotto pie, or a crispy poppadom filled with beef curry. Enjoy these dishes and the tempting dessert menu between 12.00-14.00 and 19.15-21.30 each day, but beware, there is no cooked food on Sunday evenings! Car parking is adequate and there is also a car park adjacent to the canal nearby. Walkers may leave their cars with permission. Tel 0252 617490.

Walk 8

Distance: *Allow three hours for this walk of five miles*

Suitably refreshed, leave the Barley Mow behind, cross the road and take the route through the car park and on to the tow path of the Basingstoke Canal. Turn left around the concrete slipway and follow the pleasant canal-side path. Willows grace the right-hand bank while to the left the Dogmersfield road flits behind deciduous woodland. Enjoy this wooded section passing to the left of two wooden gates before the trees begin to ease their grip. Between the two gates look out for the remains of bridge abutments, formerly the attractively named Chatter Alley Bridge, unrestored unlike the others. Before you reach Blacksmiths Bridge, restored in 1976, you will see the placid waters of Tundry Pond on your right which was enlarged to its present size by Sir Henry Milmay around 1800. On your left you will see that the land drops sharply away from the canal bank. This caused problems in 1983 when there was a landslip needing 5,000 tons of fill material carried in barges to solve the problem. As you reach Blacksmiths Bridge, leave the canal and cross the bridge which was in a poor state when restoration got under way in the mid-seventies and practically needed rebuilding.

Proceed over a stile by a wooden gate and follow the path round to the right to reach the banks of the Tundry Pond. Roughly 20 acres in extent, this large expanse of water sets nicely into a parkland background and is attractively open in character. Coots and tufted duck browsed on its still blue waters as we followed a well defined path to a three arched parkland bridge, partially under the shade of a plane tree. Turn abruptly left, away from the bridge and cross a stile right-handed of a wooden gate. Proceed along a fenced path with the broad brick facade of Dogmersfield House sitting atop a low hill a little to your left. Look for a stile on the right and take the left of two paths offered to you as you cross. When we passed, both paths were clearly visible and hopefully, you will also find this so. From the stile, head obliquely left uphill to a track which you follow right-handed still uphill past a black barn and an oil storage tank on your right. The track then takes you downhill under a high voltage transmission line and past the private fishing of Dogmersfield Lake to the right. After another track joins yours from the right, proceed over a track crossing and look for a footpath sign on your right after passing the substantial looking South Lodge. Turn right and follow this path into woodland where wellies or stout boots will be welcome as you negotiate numerous muddy areas. This woodland path leads straight ahead and, ignoring a path going left at right angles to your own, arrive at a metal gate. Do not pass through the gate but follow the path hard round to the left. With a view of the Basingstoke Canal on the right, proceed through trees to Broad Oak Bridge which you cross and turn right-handed down on to the canal's towing path. Broad Oak Bridge was a derelict eyesore when restoration work began and was completely rebuilt in 1980. Renovation of all these canal bridges was carried out using the Whitehill Brick and Tile works at Arborfield near Reading where the original bricks were obtained for the canal structures.

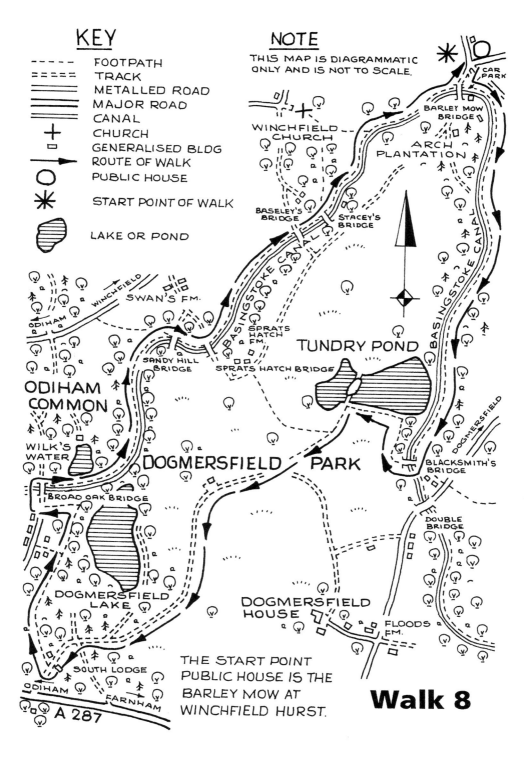

Walk 8

KEY

- - - - - FOOTPATH
===== TRACK
——— METALLED ROAD
——— MAJOR ROAD
——— CANAL
+ CHURCH
▢ GENERALISED BLDG
→ ROUTE OF WALK
◯ PUBLIC HOUSE

✳ START POINT OF WALK

◉ LAKE OR POND

NOTE

THIS MAP IS DIAGRAMMATIC ONLY AND IS NOT TO SCALE.

WINCHFIELD CHURCH

BARLEY MOW BRIDGE

CAR PARK

ARCH PLANTATION

BASINGSTOKE CANAL

BASELEY'S BRIDGE

STACEY'S BRIDGE

WINCHFIELD

SWAN'S FM.

ODIHAM

SANDY HILL BRIDGE

SPRATS HATCH FM.

SPRATS HATCH BRIDGE

TUNDRY POND

ODIHAM COMMON

WILK'S WATER

DOGMERSFIELD   PARK

DOGMERSFIELD

BLACKSMITH'S BRIDGE

BROAD OAK BRIDGE

DOUBLE BRIDGE

DOGMERSFIELD LAKE

DOGMERSFIELD HOUSE

FLOODS FM.

SOUTH LODGE

ODIHAM

FARNHAM

A 287

THE START POINT PUBLIC HOUSE IS THE BARLEY MOW AT WINCHFIELD HURST.

Barley Mow Bridge on the Basingstoke Canal

As we passed along the canal path towards Sandy Hill Bridge, the sun glinting in the trees dappled the canal's muddy waters and a moorhen called loudly to her chicks, leading them to safety in the lee of the far bank. She would have to contend with more dangers when a canal pleasure cruiser passed us at Sprats Hatch Bridge lower down on its way up to Colt Hill Wharf at Odiham. Sandy Hill and Sprats Hatch Bridges are within hailing distance of each other and both were restored in 1975. A little way past Sandy Hill Bridge we found a particularly fine clump of yellow water iris growing by the water's edge.

A further brace of bridges occurs at Baseley's and Stacey's both of which carry public footpaths over the canal, and like the previous two, both were restored in 1975. The final stretch of canal to Barley Mow Bridge is open and enjoyable. A flock of Canada geese appreciated being fed by two ladies out for a stroll and a goat eyed us nonchalantly from the garden of a picturesque timber framed cottage on the far bank. Moorhens and mallards lazily enjoyed the sunshine on the canal waters.

All too soon you are back at your starting point. Barley Mow Bridge has no restoration date on its plaque, although it is obvious that some work has been carried out. On the far side of the bridge you will find an interesting information panel about the canal and a few minutes perusal is well worth while. On the other side of the canal is the Cafe Chat Noir if you fancy a cup of tea and a browse in the adjoining gift and antiques shop. Otherwise return to the Barley Mow and your car.

Sandy wastes and cool waters from Church Crookham

WALK 9
Allow 3 ½ hours
5 ½ miles
Walk begins page 55

Background to the Walk

Within the general conurbation of the Upper Blackwater Valley are pockets of pine and heathland which offer themselves as a relief from the housing and industry of the area. It was not by chance that people were attracted to live in the pinelands of the district over the past century to enjoy the countryside and perhaps commute to London, or find employment in the surrounding rapidly developing area. This attraction may well have happened in spite of the move of the British Army to Aldershot in 1854 and the subsequent influx of tradespeople and ancillary businesses as a result. Such an attraction to the pine clad district resulted in the development of Fleet and its southern neighbour Church Crookham. The scent of fresh pine can be purchased in sprays and bottles for our homes, but here the fragrance of pine woods may be savoured by just wandering outdoors.

Fleet, which borders on this walk is a town of Victorian origins. In 1878 several acres of land were sold to a property developer form nearby Farnborough and a housing estate was planned in American style with roads laid out in grid pattern. the area on which Fleet now stands was known as 'Fuglemere' meaning a wild fowl lake. 'Fuglemere' is still there in the guise of Fleet Pond which remains a pleasant expanse of water owned by the Council and preserved for wildlife. Separating Fleet from Church Crookham is more water, this time as a ribbon of water threading its way through the houses, called the Basingstoke Canal which was there for the best part of a century before the houses arrived. This thirty-seven-and-a-half mile long waterway ex-

Maps
Landranger 1:50,000
Sheet 186
Pathfinder 1:25,000
Sheet 1205 SU 85/95
Map Reference of Start/
Finish SU826527

How to get there
From Farnham take A287 towards Odiham turning right to join B3013. At the roundabout in Church Crookham, turning right into Aldershot Road. The Foresters is on your left after half a mile. From Camberley take A325 through Farnborough turning right on to A323 towards Fleet. After one-and-a-half miles look for the turn off to Church Crookham along Aldershot Road to your left. The Foresters lies on your right-hand side about half a mile further on. Buses do not pass The Foresters, but many services pass the roundabout at Church Crookham cross roads, about half a mile from the pub. Tillingbourne regular services F11 & F12 from Aldershot, and F13 from Farnborough pass at hourly intervals. Services connect Farnham with Aldershot Bus Station where you can join F11 & F12, while Stagecoach services 20, 20A, 24 and 24A link Camberley with Farnborough (Kingsmead) to join F13.

The Foresters pub at Church Crookham

Pub facilities
Foresters,
Church Crookham
Situated just to the east of the last of the houses of Church Crookham, the Foresters is a pleasant whitewashed building standing close to the Aldershot road in a sylvan setting. It has a tiled verandah across its frontage with signs in green and gold. The landlord assured us that the inn sign showing two military men is quite wrong and that it should really display green-clad forest labourers as originally the building comprised two forester's cottages. It is smart and clean inside with upholstered chairs and a patterned carpet. To the right of the spacious main bar is the rather bare public bar, while left up the steps is the garden bar. This popular pub is open for twelve hours every day except Sunday when normal times operate. Food is served between 12.00-14.00 and 18.00-21.30 (19.00-21.30 on Sundays). Cream teas and sandwiches can be obtained at other times. An Original Country Pies menu offers Lite bites including prawn cocktail and a mushroom dipper. There is a good selection of grills, platters, sandwiches and salads, backed by a selection of Original Country Pies, including Desperate Dan Pie containing succulent pieces of beef braised in Burton Ale. In addition to all this, a specials board offers many tasty dishes from Tandoori Kebabs to Foresters Mixed Grill. Those with a thirst can sample guest ales like Tetley Bitter, Ind Coop Burton or Davenport (Changes every 3-4 weeks).

tended from the river wey at New Haw as far as Basingstoke and was opened to barge traffic in 1796. 29 locks were needed, the majority being in Surrey where the canal rises and passes through Deepcut. It is generally a maximum of 10 metres wide, although much less at some points and an average of a little over one metre deep. Although it fell out of use earlier this century, the Surrey and Hampshire Canal Society, aided by willing volunteers, restored the waterway in the late 1970s and 1980s and opened the canal to pleasure boats and the walking public. At Pondtail Bridge you may see the dredger Perseverance moored at the canal side. This venerable dredger was built in 1934 and finally completed the restoration of the Hampshire section of the canal in March 1993 after 18 years hard labour.

Most of the walk is through lands owned by the Military. The public are allowed to walk over most of these lands but must heed the posted warnings. You are frequently warned about the danger of loud noise emitting from this Military territory. The walk passes around the periphery of Long Valley and you may see the Army vehicles including tanks on exercise in the sandy, pine dotted wastes.

Adjacent to the Canal section of the walk lies the Farnborough Aerospace Centre with its testing grounds and runways. This was the birthplace of aviation in this country. Samuel Francis Cody was born in Birdville,

Claycart Bridge — built by the Army

Friary Meux Best and John Bull Bitter are regulars. If you prefer lager, there is Skol, Lowenbrau and Castlemaine. Old English Cider, Guinness and wines on tap complete the picture. A pleasant garden contains children's amusements and an aviary. Car parking is ample and pub users can leave their cars with permission. Tel 0252 616503.

Texas and first arrived in England in 1890. He was an entertainer and thrilled Music Hall audiences with his Wild West shows and actually developed a man-lifting kite in his show The Golden Nugget. He developed the kite theory and crossed the Channel in a canoe towed by a kite! The Army at Aldershot became interested in his exploits and adopted the manned kite idea in 1906 and employed him as chief kite instructor at Farnborough, making the first powered flight at the 1908 Air Show. Unfortunately Cody came to grief in a flying accident over Laffins Plain at Aldershot in 1913.

In parallel with the development of kite flying, the Army was also using manned balloons for artillery spotting and His Majesty's Balloon factory was moved to Farnborough in 1906. Development of the present Aerospace Centre was rapid and from 1911 it was used for the manufacture of aircraft. In 1914 the site was divided in offices and laboratories where testing and experiments took place. More land was acquired for runways and viewing areas for the popular and spectacular air displays in the Autumn of alternate years. The Centre now contains the oldest building in the world used continuously for aeronautical activities.

Walk 9

Distance: *Allow three-and-a-half hours for this walk of five-and-a-half miles*

If you peer into the hedge of the second car park area on the pub's left-hand side, you will discover a path leading out on to heathland. Take this and bear left through rough grassland taking up a course parallel with the road. When you see a track controlled by a vehicle barrier on the far side of the road, take a well worn path over the bank, cross the road and join the track. At two track crossings, keep straight ahead and as your route bends left you will see the Tweseldown Race Course on your right. This is a military course and used for their sporting activities, although the racing fraternity is allowed to use it in preparation for steeplechase events. On the day we passed there was no equestrian activity so we pressed on ignoring all paths on the left.

You will soon see the first warning about the danger of loud noises emitting from these military lands, but the only noise we could hear was the harsh calling of a crow in surrounding trees. Look out for the crossing of the Gelvert Stream which, at best, seems to be a mere water filled ditch. Shortly your track crosses another but proceed ahead to a second track crossing and here turn right. Directions are a little complicated hereabouts so follow the instructions carefully and don't get lost. Look for a reedy, rather murky pond on your left over which dragonflies hover. There is a confusion of tracks ahead made by Army vehicles, but keep to the left where tracks on the right converge and diverge. Even after three weeks warm, dry weather, a puddle completely spanned the track and we had to take avoiding action.

You now meet a very wide sandy track which goes around the periphery of the Long Valley training area and is used by Army vehicles as a type of distribution and access route. Go left on this track and follow its wide sandy route past a spot where you can see the testing ground on the steep slope of Long Hill. As you proceed on this track you will almost certainly encounter Army trucks driven at speed over the bumps by young men enjoying the drive! The perimeter track you are on circles the south and east sides of Long Valley and Eelmoor Plain so your route is biased towards the left. Soon, on your right, a particularly arid open area appears. No wonder the Army were offered the land in 1854 — it is useless for any kind of productive farming with the possible exception of Setaside!

At this point, your track becomes an ocean of churned up sand with two marooned islands of pine in the centre. Keep on the right-hand verge and don't worry — better things are ahead! At the far end, follow a narrow track downwards and continue on this sunken sandy track until it veers sharply left. Some time before this, you will have noticed a couple of parallel metalled roads through the pines on your right and as the track you are following takes a bend to the left, carry on straight ahead on a lesser track. This shortly tends to fizzle out and as it does so, turn right to join the nearer of the roads. These are training roads for drivers of light military vehicles. Go left and soon join the Fleet to Aldershot road.

Cross the main road and follow the footway right-handed over the Claycart Stream and take a path left directly after a cross roads sign. Cut across some open ground to join an unmetalled road which crosses the Basingstoke Canal by way of a substantial steel girder bridge with a footbridge cantilevered on the left-hand side. Turn left on the far side to join the canal tow path turning right-handed along it. After the sand of Long Valley, it is a pleasant change of environment to walk alongside the still, cool waters. Many fishermen were spending a peaceful day attempting to land perch, bream or roach while blue dragonflies enjoyed the sunshine. One young fisherman advised me that there were 'loads of perch' in the canal and that huge pike stalk the depths. Water bailiffs check for permits.

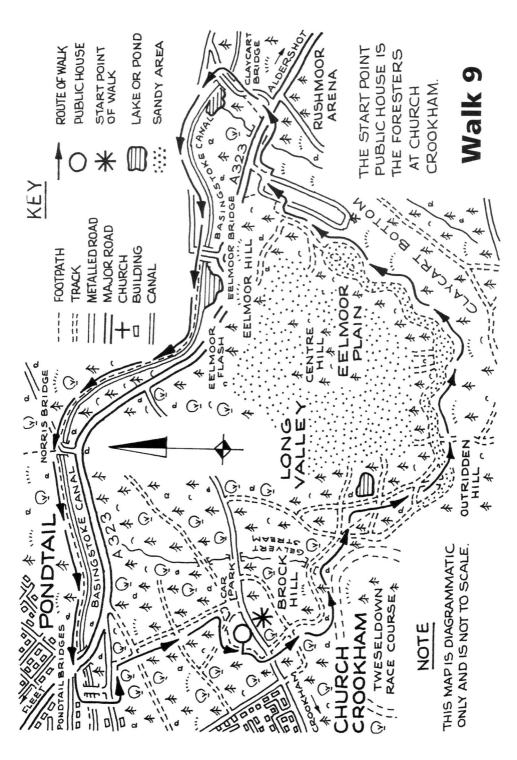

Walk 9

KEY

- - - - FOOTPATH
- - - - TRACK
===== METALLED ROAD
===== MAJOR ROAD
✝ ⌂ CHURCH BUILDING
===== CANAL

→ ROUTE OF WALK
○ PUBLIC HOUSE
✳ START POINT OF WALK
▭ LAKE OR POND
⸬ SANDY AREA

THE START POINT PUBLIC HOUSE IS THE FORESTERS AT CHURCH CROOKHAM.

NOTE

THIS MAP IS DIAGRAMMATIC ONLY AND IS NOT TO SCALE.

On the noisier side, further along, a fighter jet roared and boomed off from the main runway of the Royal Aerospace Centre guarded by high wire fencing on the right. There were marsh marigolds and horseshoe vetch on the canal bank while coots and moorhens paddled contentedly in the water. Continue along the canal under the steel girdered Eelmoor Bridge followed after some distance by the high concrete Norris Bridge, until you reach the bridges at Pondtail. If you are tall, stoop low under the first bridge and then follow a tarmac path right-handed to turn and cross the second bridge. The dredger Perseverance stood idle on the canal after completing canal dredging in March 1993.

After crossing the bridge turn left on the roadway and then right along a well worn path to a crossing of tracks. Take the track opposite which leads straight through mainly pine

Norris Bridge on the Basingstoke Canal

woodland until you hear the sound of traffic as you approach a T-junction of tracks with a vehicle barrier on the right. Just before this, look for a path on the right which passes to the rear of a gravelled car park and then leads over a cross track with another vehicle barrier on your left. As another track joins from the right, proceed uphill and turn right at a junction at the rear of The Foresters pub. Where a path branches left past the pub's garden, follow this and enter the car park by the way you left it earlier.

Clear chalk waters and a Royal castle from Odiham

Background to the Walk

Odiham is a delightful little town standing in the valley of the Whitewater with the chalk ridge of the North Downs to the south. The meaning of the name is simply 'a wooded homestead or enclosure'. There is nothing special about this derivation but there is something special about the fine Georgian façades which line the spacious High Street. All are neat and well-tended, which urges the passer-by to leave their car and admire the town more closely on foot. At the time of Domesday it had eight mills and four churches and a population of 247 — the second largest in Hampshire after Winchester. Next to the church is a fine set of stocks and a whipping post, with the iron arm-clamps still to be seen. Odiham is not all ancient history, as to the south of the town is Odiham airfield, an RAF station built in 1937 and still operational with most of the original buildings intact. On July 15th 1953, Odiham staged the biggest flypast ever mounted by the RAF when it celebrated the Coronation of Queen Elizabeth, with over 640 aircraft taking part in the review.

On the walk you will suddenly come across Odiham Castle, a gaunt and shapeless ruin with huge gaping holes for windows. Since Saxon times, Odiham has been a Royal Manor and was a convenient stopping place between the castles of Windsor and Winchester. King John, who reigned between 1199 and 1216 ordered a castle to be built and this was done between 1207 and 1214. It was built of flint and is the only remaining octagonal castle in the country. John spent much time at the castle hunting in the locality during his troubled reign and it was from Odiham castle that

Maps
Landranger 1:50,000
Sheet 186
Pathfinder 1:25,000
Sheet 1204 SU65/75
Map Reference of Start/
Finish SU746516

How to get there
From Farnham take A287 towards Odiham taking the first left exit on the roundabout on the eastern side of the town. Proceed towards the town and take the first turning right (the old London Road). The Water Witch is tucked away to your left before you reach the canal bridge. From Camberley follow A30 westwards through Hartley Wintney. At Phoenix Green, beyond the village, take B3016 on your left signed Winchfield and Odiham. When you reach A287 (Odiham by pass) turn left and then go right handed at the roundabout to enter Odiham. Proceed as above. From Farnham Altonian Coaches service 207 runs via Crondall to Odiham, but it is a restricted service so check with the company on 0420 84839. Alternatively you can use Hampshire Bus regular services 214 and 215 to Alton and change to service 201 run by Relief Coaches. Again this is a restricted service so check on 0252 617614. When you

alight, look for the old London Road on the east side of the town and walk down to the Water Witch. From Camberley the Hampshire Bus regular service 200 between there and Basingstoke passes through Odiham at hourly intervals.

Pub facilities
Water Witch,
Colt Hill, Nr Odiham
Standing discreetly back from the old London Road, the Water Witch is a character pub with a pleasing frontage. The oldest parts date back 500 years, as old as the ancient well which graces the main bar. The pub interior is low beamed, interesting and full of snug corners with a multitude of copperware utensils. You can savour this antiquity between the hours of 11.00-14.30 and 18.00-23.00 (Mon-Sat), 12.00-15.00 and 19.00-22.30 (Sun). During the six weeks of the summer school holidays the pub is open all day (11.00-23.00). The pub is one of the South Coast Taverns group and when we called was serving Ruddles County and a guest ale (Youngs Bitter). If you are a pensioner there is a Pensioner's Special lunch, but it must be ordered between 11.30-12.30. Food serving times are between 11.30-14.00 and 18.00-21.00 (Mon-Sat), 12.00-14.30 and 19.00-21.00 on Sundays. Beyond the main bar is a family room leading out to a large garden stretching down to the canal bank. Ducks may want to share your meal if you eat outside but in compensation there are many amusements for the children. The car park is not large, but walkers may

The Water Witch at Colt Hill near Odiham

he emerged with his entourage to ride, in foul mood, to sign the Magna Carta at Runnymede.

The Dauphin of France sent troops over to England in 1216 to support the barons and Odiham Castle was besieged. Its garrison of 13 men held out for 15 days, much to the amazement of the Dauphin's troops. Following this, Simon de Montfort, that father of the British Parliament, married John's daughter Eleanor and together they spent happy times while residing at the castle. During the problems with Henry III, Simon was killed at the battle of Evesham, and after 30 happy years of marriage, his grieving widow left Odiham to reside at Portchester Castle. From then on, the castle declined, although Edward I — the 'Hammer of the Scots — imprisoned King David of Scotland there for several years early in the 14th century. So the castle had a lively but relatively short life as such and its stark ruins are now in the care of Hants County Council.

The Basingstoke Canal is a feature of this walk and the tow path is followed right up to the eastern portal of the Greywell Tunnel. A grill bars further progress and protects the home of several species of bats, including the rare Natterer bat. Only one site in Poland exceeds the numbers of this species here and apart from the Natterers, there are four other bat types. Over 500 bats have been recorded at one time and there could be over 12,000 bats in the tunnel, so don't investigate the entrance too closely at dusk! The brick-arched tunnel was built circa 1792 and took the canal under Greywell Hill, a distance of 1230 yards. Bargees lay on their backs and propelled the barge along by walking on the tunnel roof. As with many canal tunnels, a lack of maintenance led to a roof fall which has blocked the tunnel since 1932. Enthusiasts would like to reopen the tunnel but the cost of repairs would be formidable and would achieve little, as the line of the canal west of Mapledurwell has been confused by the new roads and buildings of Basingstoke. It would be better to leave the bats in peace! The last barge to traverse the whole length of the canal, all 37·5 miles of it between New Haw in Surrey and Basingstoke, was in 1914 and after this, use of the canal slumped — although during the first World War it was frequently used on the Surrey section up to Aldershot. A. J. Harmsworth acquired the canal in 1923 and actually increased usage up to 1935 by barge building and by promoting trade, but after his death, traffic on the canal effectively ceased.

leave their vehicles if permission is asked.
Tel 0256 702778.

Swan,
Odiham
This broad-fronted pub with its white façade lies just to the north of Swan Bridge which carries the B3349 over the Basingstoke Canal. A warm, welcoming pub, it has a good local trade as well as attracting passing custom. The building dates back over 500 years and has always been a pub. Opening times are between 11.00-14.30 and 18.00-23.00 (Mon-sat) and the usual times for Sunday. Food can be ordered between 12.00-14.30 and 19.00-21.00 seven days a week. The Swan is a free house and serves up Marstons Pedigree, Courage Best, Ruddles County and Wadworth 6X. Food is very varied with a menu and specials board. There is a pleasant garden (with childrens amusements) and a large car park.
Tel 0256 702727.

As early as 1932, the Surrey and Hampshire Canal Society put forward proposals to renovate the canal but it was not until the late 1970s that work finally commenced. Now walkers can enjoy the canal and look out for the 27 species of dragonfly which hover over the water and see the many aquatic plants which flourish in and around the canal.

Walk 10

Distance: *Allow three-and-a-half hours for this walk of five-and-a-half miles.*
Leave the pub and turn left towards Colt Hill Canal Bridge, noting on your left the old Cricketers Inn. High up on the gable end, a plaque reads *Crowley and Co. Alton, Ales and Stouts*, an echo from bygone times when small breweries thrived in these hop growing lands. Proceed over the canal bridge and turn left on to the towing path. Colt Hill Bridge was probably built in 1792 and was restored in the mid-1970s. The path leads through an attractive pastoral landscape up to Lodge Copse Bridge which is a simple affair without sides. A barge was being loaded with gravel as we passed to improve the towing path, principally for the maintenance

vehicles. Further along, the bank contains many flowering grasses, dropwort, yellow water iris and similarly coloured marsh marigolds. To enhance this, as the canal swings into a left-hand curve, the River Whitewater comes into view on your right, its crystal clear waters winding through lush meadowland. Soon you pass under Swan Bridge and if you have worked up an early thirst or an appetite, the attractive Swan Inn beckons from the road above.

You will find the canal waters becoming evermore clear as you walk along and on them we saw two swans accompanied by five cygnets — the male taking time off to chase a mallard away. Pass to the right of a wooden gate and with cottages on your right, approach the North Warnborough Lift Bridge which takes a narrow lane over the canal. Cross the lane and rejoin the path, looking out for the ruins of Odiham Castle on your right and spare time to look around King John's Castle, its flint walls still resisting the ravages of time. Cross over the River Whitewater by means of a small aqueduct and soon you will see a turning point for vessels, as a boom prevents further progress on the water. The final stretch to the Greywell Tunnel portal is weed girt, but the waters are clear and were being enjoyed by a family of coots as we passed by. There is a grill just inside the portal but we could see nothing of the bats who make the tunnel their home.

Leave the canal, perhaps regretfully and walk up to a junction of signed paths where you go right and pass to the right of a metal gate. Cross over an access track with another gate on your right and pass through a V-shaped stile with a lifting arm to the left of the second gate. V-shaped stiles are not often encountered in the South, but are common in the North and called 'snicket' stiles, where very often the separate V-pieces are formed out of monolithic gritstone.

With a barn on your right, pass around the corner of a brick building to find a stile which you cross to proceed along the left hand edge of a meadow to another stile. Angle slightly left along a defined path to cross over another V stile into Hook Road at its junction with Dorchester Way. Follow Hook Road right-handed past houses until you see a track entering a field to your right with a V stile in the hedge to the left of the gap. We looked in vain for a footpath sign, but I can assure you that it is a right of way. Pass through the gap and turn left to follow a grassy field edge track past the rear of a quaint thatched cottage and continue parallel with Hook Road through a pair of closely set V stiles. Maintain your direction along left-hand field edges until you reach another V stile on the edge of woodland. Negotiate the stile by a three-armed footpath sign and turn right along a well-trodden, tree-shaded path. As the path divides take either one as they soon meet again just before an overgrown pond on the left. The same thing happens again but you soon leave the woodland behind to join in turn, a gravel access road and a metalled lane by Webbs Cottage. Follow the lane left-handed and take the right-hand fork as it reaches houses. Go right again at the next junction and follow the lane as it swings left to join B3349 at the top end of North Warnborough.

Your route lies across the road and over a stile to the left of a metal gate. Before you do this, stand on the bridge to your right and pause a few seconds to admire

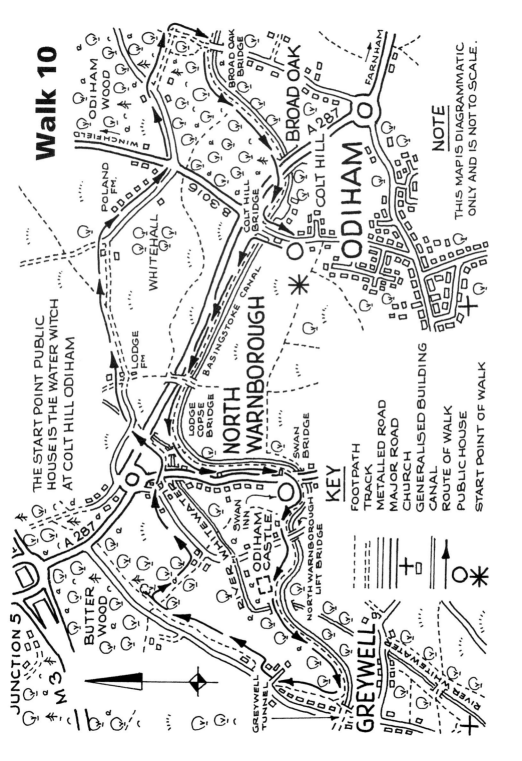

Walk 10

THE START POINT PUBLIC HOUSE IS THE WATER WITCH AT COLT HILL ODIHAM

NOTE

THIS MAP IS DIAGRAMMATIC ONLY AND IS NOT TO SCALE.

KEY

FOOTPATH	
TRACK	
METALLED ROAD	
MAJOR ROAD	
CHURCH	
GENERALISED BUILDING	
CANAL	
ROUTE OF WALK	
PUBLIC HOUSE	
START POINT OF WALK	

ODIHAM WOOD

WINCHFIELD

POLAND FM.

WHITEHALL

LODGE FM.

BROAD OAK BRIDGE

BROAD OAK

COLT HILL

A 287

FARNHAM

ODIHAM

COLT HILL BRIDGE

BASINGSTOKE CANAL

NORTH WARNBOROUGH

LODGE COPSE BRIDGE

SWAN BRIDGE

JUNCTION 5

M 3

A 287

BUTTER WOOD

WHITEWATER

RIVER

SWAN INN

ODIHAM CASTLE

NORTH WARNBOROUGH LIFT BRIDGE

GREYWELL TUNNEL

GREYWELL

RIVER WHITEWATER

The romantic ruins of Odiham Castle

the Old Mill House which is now a restaurant, overlooking the clear waters of the River Whitewater. Resume your walk and follow a concrete road near the river on your right. Soon your path is joined by another from the right over a footbridge. From here the path is ill-defined but follow the river bank to a stile to the right of a wooden gate as you approach the Odiham by-pass. With the river to your right, cross the stile and go right under the new bridge where you veer right, over a stile to join a concrete road which you follow straight ahead to Lodge Farm. This farm has PYO fruit fields and amateur strawberry pickers were numerous when we did this walk. As you approach the farm, veer slightly right past the car park and the fenced pond heading for the right-hand side of brick cottages, where you will find a gate and a footpath sign. From here follow a wide gravelled farm road under power lines until you meet the metalled Poland Lane where you turn right, passing Poland Farm and other attractive cottages before crossing London Road into Bagwell Lane.

After Bagwell Lane swings gently left, look out for a footpath sign on the right after you have passed the entrance to Derrydown. This is a track which takes you into the woodland of Odiham Common where oaks, holly and hazel predominate. When you reach a lesser-used cross track, turn right and follow this often muddy track back to the Basingstoke Canal at Broad Oak Bridge. Go left down to the canal path and then right under the bridge following the tow path under the by-pass bridge back to Colt Hill Bridge and the Water Witch.

Fine parkland and a hill top castle from Heath End

WALK 11
Allow 4 hours
6 miles
Walk begins page 68

Background to the Walk

The houses of Heath End, Hale and Hog Hatch, mark the southern end of the Aldershot and Blackwater Valley conurbation. Significantly it ends on a high note with Bricksbury Hill, Sandy Hill and Hungry Hill forming a sandy escarpment overlooking the flatter lands of Farnborough, Fleet and Cove. On a spur of Bricksbury Hill stands the iron age fort of Caesars Camp which from afar is a prominent landmark with a handful of pines on its lofty summit. Heath End is really a part of hill top Hale which is separated from Farnham to the south by the rolling green lands of Farnham Park. Hale has lost its peacefulness of yester-year and today heavy traffic rumbles through its heart — but the heart still beats around the pleasant green bordering the main road where the village men were renowned for their football and cricket teams. 'The men from the hill' they were called. Albert Baker learned how to play a straight bat on this green and went on to form a solid opening partnership with Surrey's greatest cricketing son, Sir Jack Hobbs, in the early years of this century.

Hale is quite a common name meaning 'a place in the nook or corner of land', but the nearby Farnham takes its meaning from 'a homestead or enclosure where ferns grow'. Farnham lies in an interesting geological position astride a fault line severing Hampshire's North Downs from the narrow chalk ridge of the Hogs Back. In recent geological times, the north branch of the River Wey formed the head waters of the present River Blackwater thus truncating that part of the River Wey which flows past Waverley Abbey to join the Wey's

Maps
Landranger 1:50,000
Sheet 186.
Pathfinder 1:25,000
Sheet 1225 SU84/94
Map Reference of Start/
Finish SU844494.

How to get there
From Farnham join A325 and head towards Farnborough passing Hale Church and after this turning left into Alma Lane (B3005) at the traffic lights at Heath End cross roads. The Alma is a quarter of a mile on your left. From Camberley take A325 southbound through Farnborough and past the turn offs to Aldershot until you reach the traffic lights at Heath End. Turn right here into Alma Lane (B3005) and after a quarter of a mile locate the Alma on your left. Stagecoach services 14 and 15 together with Guildford and West Surrey service 552 pass the Alma en route between Farnham and Aldershot. From Camberley take Stagecoach services 20, 20A, 24 or 24A to Aldershot bus station and change on to Stagecoach services 14 or 15 to Farnham which pass the Alma.

Pub facilities
Alma,
Heath End
*In an urban area the Alma Inn
shows up attractively in its
dressing of flint infill and
brick quoins with sash
windows, hanging baskets and
flower pots providing a splash
of colour. Inside, the pub is
quite plain but pleasant and
carpeted. There is a public bar
(with pool table) and a saloon
bar, but these two are to be
changed over under the
landlord's ambitious scheme
to improve the pub further. It
is over 150 years old and
commemorates the battle of the
Alma in the Crimean War
where 2,200 Allied Soldiers
died. Trade has trebled since
the present landlord took over
in 1992 and as well as plans
for the interior, he intends to
expand the present small,
willow-shaded garden at the
rear. Even now there are
chldren's amusements and a
few tables. Formerly a
Courage House, it has now
been taken over by Morlands
and serves Old Speckled Hen,
Old Masters Original Bitter
and Revival Dark Mild. The
guest ale is Bass and there are
two draught lagers. All this
can be sampled from 11.00-
23.00 with normal opening
times on Sunday. Appetites
are satisfied by a menu and a
specials board — the latter
offering vegetarian lasagne
and mushrooms with garlic
ravioli when we called.
Everything is home cooked
and available during opening
times. Walkers should ask
permission to leave their cars.
Tel 0252 20978.*

The Alma at Heath End

southern branch at Tilford. The present watershed
between the Blackwater and the Wey east of Farnham
is very low indeed. Before the Normans arrived, a
great battle was fought in the Farnham area between
Alfred, King of Wessex and the Danish invaders in AD
896. The Danes had pillaged parts of what is now
Berkshire and Hampshire but Alfred brought them up
with a jolt with a decisive victory, forcing them to
retreat.

Henry of Blois, a grandson of William the Con-
queror and brother of the hapless King Stephen has
much involvement in the history of Farnham. It was
Henry who built Farnham Castle in 1138, commanding as it does the Wey valley from its hill, and it was he
who planned the medieval townscape of Farnham.
The Castle was the official seat of the Bishops of
Winchester until 1927. The Keep is open to the public
daily, but public admittance to the great hall and other
rooms is restricted to Wednesdays between 14.00-
16.00. The grand approach to the castle from the town
is by way of Castle Street with its elegant Georgian
façades. Originally designed to be wide enough to
accommodate markets and fairs, it is, without doubt,
the finest street in Farnham.

The town's prosperity in the Middle Ages came
from the cloth trade and until the 17th century it was an
important wool market. Later the hop flower paid a
great part in Farnham's fortunes and the town at one

Waynflete's Tower at Farnham Castle

Nelson Arms,
Castle St, Farnham
This fine old white fronted pub stands in Farnham's most attractive thoroughfare, the wide, sloping Castle Street. Dating from the 15th Century it was originally four cottages tied to the local Maltings (now a Craft Centre). The interior is timbered with low ceilings and pictures of Nelson's last battle — see if you can find a glass eye set into one of the beams! The pub is open 12 hours each day with the usual Sunday opening times. Food is available each day between 12.00-14.30 and 17.30-19.30 (but later on Thursday and Fridays). No food is served Sunday evenings. There is no car park so walkers would need to park in the town, as Castle Street parking is limited to 2 hours. Courage beers and John Smiths are on tap with Wadworth 6X as a guest ale. There are three choices for lager lovers.
Tel 0252 716078.

time boasted five brewers. The Wey valley from Alton and then eastwards of Farnham was fine hop growing country. Hop picking must have been a lively time in the old days when local hop pickers in their thousands took to the fields together with gypsies and other itinerant workers. Seven-bushel baskets were used for picking the hops, a country industry which was in its heyday in the late 19th and early 20th centuries. Hops figured in the Great Exhibition of 1851 in Hyde Park, when a Mr Eliot of Farnham exhibited a model of his new-fangled bagging machine.

No word about Farnham is complete without mention of a favourite son. William Cobbett the reformist, radical politician, diarist and author was born in 1762 at the Jolly Farmer in Bridge Square. He was the son of a farm labourer and helped on the land but studied keenly in his spare time. He founded a respected journal, the *Political Register*, in 1802. He served in the Army and denounced the service for some of the barbaric punishments meted out to the common soldier. Later he suffered imprisonment for his political views. Perhaps his greatest legacy was his diary *Rural Rides* in which he described his travels around the country on horseback. He studied the countryside and the conditions in which ordinary people lived, putting his views and thoughts in the book which has become a classic of English literature. He became the MP for Oldham in 1832 and died in 1835 at the age of 73 at Normandy Farm north of the Hogs Back. His birthplace is now the William Cobbett pub.

Walk 11

Distance: *Allow four hours for this walk of six miles*

Leave the pub, cross the road and go left-handed past Yonder Cottage until you see a trackway on your right by the side of Beams Cottage, where a peep over the garden gate is rewarding. Where the track bears right take the path straight ahead veering left near the rear fences of estate houses with a large area of broom on your right. Climb steeply to join a track where you turn left, with houses on your left. A glance right offers commanding views over Long Bottom backed by the pine-topped hill fort of Caesars camp on Bricksbury Hill. Right of this you will see the buildings and runways of the Farnborough Aerospace Centre. A rather ugly concrete water tower appears ahead as you continue forward, ignoring all right turning tracks. At a track junction take the left hand exit around the side of a ditch, recently dug when we passed, and continue over another track until you meet a busy road. Go directly over this into a minor road called Lawday Link and as you proceed, you may catch a glimpse of Crooksbury Hill or even Leith Hill on the left from your high position. Cross A287 and enter Heathyfields Road, a poorly surfaced access road which soon narrows with pines and oaks protected by a wire fence on your right. Emerge into a close like area with new housing, keeping right on the footway and maintaining direction down a metalled access closed in by high cupressus hedges.

A couple of bends brings you to a track junction where you bear right, then immediately left down a pleasant track past Upper Old Park to meet another track opposite Woodside Cottage, where you turn right. A sign by white gates announces that this is a footpath and bridleway only. Reassured by this, follow the track down and then up past the Georgian style Middle Old Park, where your track becomes a metalled road. A double bend precedes Keepers Cottage on you right before you descend to the white gates of Lower Old Park. On this section, look over to your right to see the imposing brick facade of Ewshott Hall set upon its hillside. Follow the lane left-handed past the white gates of Lower Old Park, all this area being formerly part of the great park of Farnham Castle, and descend to a brick arched bridge, looking for a wooden pedestrian gate to the left. A metal footpath sign points your way down the valley where a leafy path takes you forward to a metalled access road. Have a peep through the hedge on your right at the fine buildings of Bulles Farm, complete with a garden waterfall, before proceeding down the lane past brick bridges and stone cottages to cross the Farnham to Crondall road.

Here you will find a wooden footpath sign where you proceed left handed obliquely up a bank, with the path straightening out to lead uphill over a meadow to a lone footpath sign on the ridge. The path was well defined over the newly mown meadows as we passed. At the top, you will find a strip of rough grass running along the ridge. Turn left on this and gradually descend, with the tall tower of Farnham Church ahead and the houses of Wrecclesham over to the right. A rainstorm curtained the heights of Hindhead beyond Wrecclesham and we

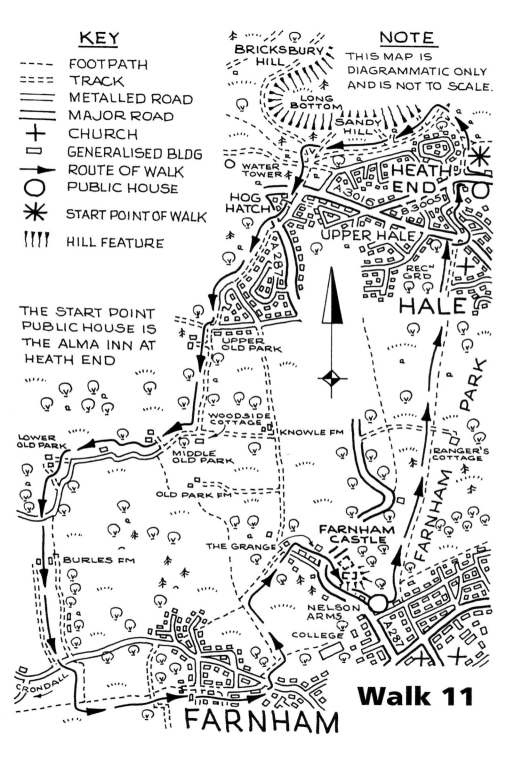

KEY

- - - - FOOTPATH
- - - - TRACK
═══ METALLED ROAD
══ MAJOR ROAD
+ CHURCH
▫ GENERALISED BLDG
→ ROUTE OF WALK
○ PUBLIC HOUSE
✳ START POINT OF WALK
|||| HILL FEATURE

NOTE

THIS MAP IS DIAGRAMMATIC ONLY AND IS NOT TO SCALE.

THE START POINT PUBLIC HOUSE IS THE ALMA INN AT HEATH END

BRICKSBURY HILL

LONG BOTTOM

SANDY HILL

WATER TOWER

HOG HATCH

HEATH END

A 3016

B 3005

UPPER HALE

REC^N GRD

HALE

A 287

FARNHAM PARK

UPPER OLD PARK

LOWER OLD PARK

WOODSIDE COTTAGE

MIDDLE OLD PARK

KNOWLE FM

OLD PARK FM

RANGER'S COTTAGE

BURLES FM

THE GRANGE

FARNHAM CASTLE

NELSON ARMS

COLLEGE

A 287

CRONDALL

FARNHAM

Walk 11

checked the brooding sky anxiously. The path bends left at the hedged corner of a field and leads down steps to a stile. Go right handed along the meadow side to another stile and after crossing this and a trackway, head down a pleasing path, over a strip of meadow and to a footbridge overhung by willows, Pause to have a look at the trick-ling waters before tack-

Cottages in Old Park Lane, Farnham

ling a stairway of concrete steps up to join a track opposite Blackbirds. Follow this left handed, cross a road and proceed down the gravelled Waynflete Lane, named after Bishop Waynflete of Winchester diocese, who once resided at Farnham Castle and has a tower gatehouse named after him. Waynfletes Lane's gravelled surface soon becomes metalled as you head down to meet the Farnham to Crondall road once again.

A footpath sign opposite and a little to the left beckons you into meadowland and you cannot stray from the well worn path through a belt of trees into another meadow before turning left handed up the hill and along the right hand field edge. When you encounter another path at the top, turn right and make your way along a hedge side path, passing a rusty old barn on your right to soon enter Old Park lane with its attendant fine cottages — Grange Cottage, The Cookhouse and Barn End which you pass as you turn right-handed into the lane. the massive, square keep-like Grange can be glimpsed on your left after passing Barn End. Pass over the A287 to join a pleasant footway set back from the road and turn right down to Farnham Castle entrance. If you wish to view the castle, deviate here and rejoin the route which descends seven flights of seven steps each into Castle Street — built wide enough to accommodate markets and fairs. Turn left by the Nelson Arms, handily placed for refreshment, to join Park Row, which initially is a narrow street with old town houses. Where the road widens, turn left at the corner of No. 17 into an alleyway signed Farnham Park. This leads you into the park where you take the left of the two metalled paths which are presented to you.

Follow this path for nearly a mile undulating through fine parkland views passing left-handed of the Park Ranger's house. As you leave the park go straight ahead past the cream-washed Sussex Cottage and Upper Hale Green to meet the main road. Cross this with care and walk up Vicarage Lane opposite to meet Heath Lane. Turn left here and then right into Alma lane to reach the pub and your car.

Ancient tracks and downland slopes from Crondall

WALK 12
Allow 3 hours
5 miles
Walk begins page 73

Background to the Walk

Just before the green downland slopes of Hampshire are transformed into the sandy gravels and pines of the Surrey border lands, we find the picturesque village of Crondall, winner of the 1993 best kept Hampshire village competition after previously winning the title in 1975 and often runner-up in the interim years. The village name derives from the Saxon 'Crundellan' which means 'place by the chalk pits' of which there have been many in the locality. The village centre, The Borough, contains many buildings of great architectural interest and the central village pub, the Plume of Feathers, is one of these. The area around Crondall was the scene of many skirmishes during the Civil War when Roundheads from Farnham Castle and Royalists from Basing House clashed in this no man's land.

There is a ghost from that war, that of a Roundhead horseman who rides along the avenue of limes up to and through the church doorway, probably to rejoin his comrades who were quartered in the church. The church of All Saints pre-dates Cromwell by nearly 500 years, some call it the finest church in Hampshire and the 'cathedral of North Hampshire'. It is built on the site of a Saxon church and is Norman in style, with fine semi-circular arches springing from the nave pillars. The tower is brick and replaced a Norman structure which became unsafe and was taken down in 1657. The church remained towerless until a replacement was built two years later — a replica of a church tower at Battersea in London which was demolished in 1775. The avenue of limes used to stretch from gate to porch but the older trees nearest the church porch had to be

Maps
Landranger 1:50,000
Sheet 186
Pathfinder 1:25,000
Sheets 1224 & 1225
SU64/74 and SU84/94
Map Reference of Start/
Finish SU795488

How to get there
From Farnham take A325 (West Street) to the junction with Crondall Lane turning right and proceeding direct to Crondall. Turn left into the Borough and look for the Plume of Feathers on your left. From Camberley take A30 westwards and turn left on to A327 just past the Ely Hotel. Turn quickly right to join B3013 and follow this until you meet A323 in Fleet. Cross directly over to join Crookham Road and follow signs for Crondall to find the Plume of Feathers on your left in the centre of the village. Altonian Coach service 207 between Farnham and Odiham passes through Crondall, while Tillingbourne service F40 from Camberley to Farnham also calls, the latter being a two-hourly service and the former a restricted service.

Pub facilities
Plume of Feathers, Crondall

This grand old coaching inn on the old route between Farnham and Basingstoke has been a pub since 1620 and lies in the heart of quaint Crondall. Its fabric is mainly 15th Century but there are parts dating from a century earlier. There are creaks and groans from the ancient woodwork and it is said that a man was once hanged in the bar. Oliver Cromwell did stay here and much is said about him on a board in the passageway. The pub is open from 11.00-15.00 and 18.00-23.00 every day except Sunday, when hours of 12.00-15.00 and 19.00-22.30 apply. Food is served all days of the week from 12.00-14.00 and 19.00-22.00 but there are no chips and no frozen food. Reasonably priced food is listed on a blackboard and there is a separate menu for the cosy restaurant on the other side of the bar. The pub is a Morland house and you can sample Morland Old Masters, Morland Original or Old Speckled Hen along with Kronenberg or Fosters lager. There is a quaint yard outside with two red telephone kiosks full of plants and a further seating area beyond the car park. Walkers may leave their cars but ask permission first. Tel 0252 850245.

The Plume of Feathers at Crondall

felled for safety reasons in 1987 after standing in line since 1759. The remaining limes were planted in 1879 when the churchyard was extended.

If you have a preference for the macabre take a look at the John Eggar memorial on the north wall of the Lady Chapel. As well as a brass plate you will also see a skeleton in a shroud. John Eggar was a local man who lived at Montgomerys Farm, which you will glimpse on this walk. He founded a free school in Alton under a trust deed in 1638 and it has survived for over 350 years seeing many changes. The free school ended in 1868 when fees were introduced.

Moving on to more modern times, you will be impressed by the fine building of Clare Park as you descend to the lowlands from the chalk ridge. It lies in the vale to your right and is a broad-fronted Georgian building, built two centuries ago by a West Indian planter called Harding, returning to his homeland with a large staff of West Indian servants. Some years ago it became a retirement complex for the active elderly. Standing in eight acres of ground with twelve bungalows for the residents, it is a fine, dominating building.

Overlooking Clare Park from a tree-shrouded knoll are the remains of a castle, passed on the walk. It stands on private land and was an ancient earthwork when the Normans took over and built Powderham Castle. A

Cottages in The Borough at Crondall

low mound and a fosse is all that remains of this stronghold which was one of the unlicensed castles of Stephen's turbulent reign. It may have been the residence of the Bishops of Winchester before they began living at the nearby Farnham Castle.

The walk follows a section of the ancient Harrow Way as it moves over the high chalkland. Although this part of the route is now metalled, it still preserves a feel of antiquity. It was a remarkable road and led from the West Country to the sea havens of Kent. Even in Anglo Saxon Charters of AD900 it was known as the 'old way' with our present day 'Harrow' being derived from 'Hor' or 'Hoar' meaning old or ancient way.

Near Powderham Castle is the Clare Park BUPA hospital which is well signed on roads in the district. It was opened in October 1980 by the chairman of British Caledonia Airways. It operates successfully and has 31 in-patient rooms and some very modern hospital equipment. Further extensions are to be considered.

Walk 12

Distance: *Allow three hours for this walk of five miles*

From the front entrance of the Plume of Feathers, step out into the picturesque Borough, turning left and left again into Church Street. The quaint brick cottages of Church Street are a fitting introduction to the substantial, brick-towered church of All Saints, with its brick-paved access path leading up to the church door by way of its shortened avenue of limes. Where Church Street meets Croft Lane, turn right past The Castle pub opposite the church. Find time to look around the church as 'the cathedral of North Hampshire' is certainly worth a few minutes of your time.

Continue along the lane past Hook Meadow, backed by its line of poplars on the right, strolling past the entrance to Farm Lane on your left and down to where the

Castle Inn, Crondall

This pub, opposite the church, was moved over a century ago when the churchyard was extended. It is a traditional village pub with one bar and a separate restaurant with a log fire to cheer you in winter. Reasonably priced food is served from 12.00-14.00 and 19.00-21.30, and to go with this you can sample Fullers ales together with Chiswick Pride and ESB. There is a garden and walkers are welcome to leave cars. The pub opens between 11.30-14.30 and 18.00-23.00 daily with usual Sunday hours. Tel 0252 850892.

Hampshire Arms, Crondall

This country village pub is noted for its food and hospitality, featuring home cooked food, Sunday roasts and a children's menu served between 12.00-14.00 and 19.00-22.00 seven days a week. The one bar is supplemented by a conservatory and a garden. Old Dray is on offer as a guest ale between the hours of 11.00-15.00 and 17.30-23.00 (Mon-Sat) with usual Sunday hours. Walkers may leave cars with permission. Tel 0252 850418.

lane turns sharply right. Proceed directly ahead on a track towards corrugated barns, turning left as you reach the entrance to them to follow an open field track with crops and cereals on either side. Where the track forks, take the right-hand route which leads gently uphill towards trees. If you look right of centre, you will see the two prominent humps of Horsedown

The Borough at Crondall

Common which reach a grassy height of 162 metres, or 541 feet if you prefer. We found a sea of bluebells and white greater stitchwort as we entered Lee Wood to follow a track left-handed, ignoring the path leading off right.

Yellow brimstone and multi-coloured peacock butterflies fluttered about as we climbed gradually through deciduous woodland, which had been cleared in some places. Shortly your path briefly emerges from the woodland with a cereal field on your left and a row of pines mixed with hawthorn on your right. A wood of hazel and oak closes in once again before your well-defined path gives way to a track with two newly built houses to the left. Follow the track until it joins a lane by the entrance to the substantial Swanthorpe House. If you look over to the right while walking this section you will see the buildings of Montgomerys Farm, once home to John Eggar, founder of Eggar's School in Alton.

Turn left on the lane continuing a steady climb to the crest of the North Downs ridge. On your way, you will notice an old deep chalk pit on the left and further along, a gap in the trees gives fine views to the north, with Crondall Church standing out very clearly. Continue along the lane until you reach a T-junction of lanes where you turn left. Before doing so, step across the road and admire the view southwards over the old hop lands of Hampshire to the wooded heights of Hindhead on the skyline. Follow the lane along the ridge top in the knowledge that countless other feet have tramped along the same route before, as it is the ancient Harrow Way, old even to the Saxons. As you proceed, with a belt of trees shielding your left-hand side, the old town of Farnham comes into view in the valley ahead backed by the conical pine topped eminence of Crooksbury Hill — fine country and fine views.

Shortly on your left, now bereft of sheltering trees, a trackway heads down to a wood in which you will find the ring motte and bailey fortress of Barley Pound probably of 12th Century construction and reputed to be the one time headquar-

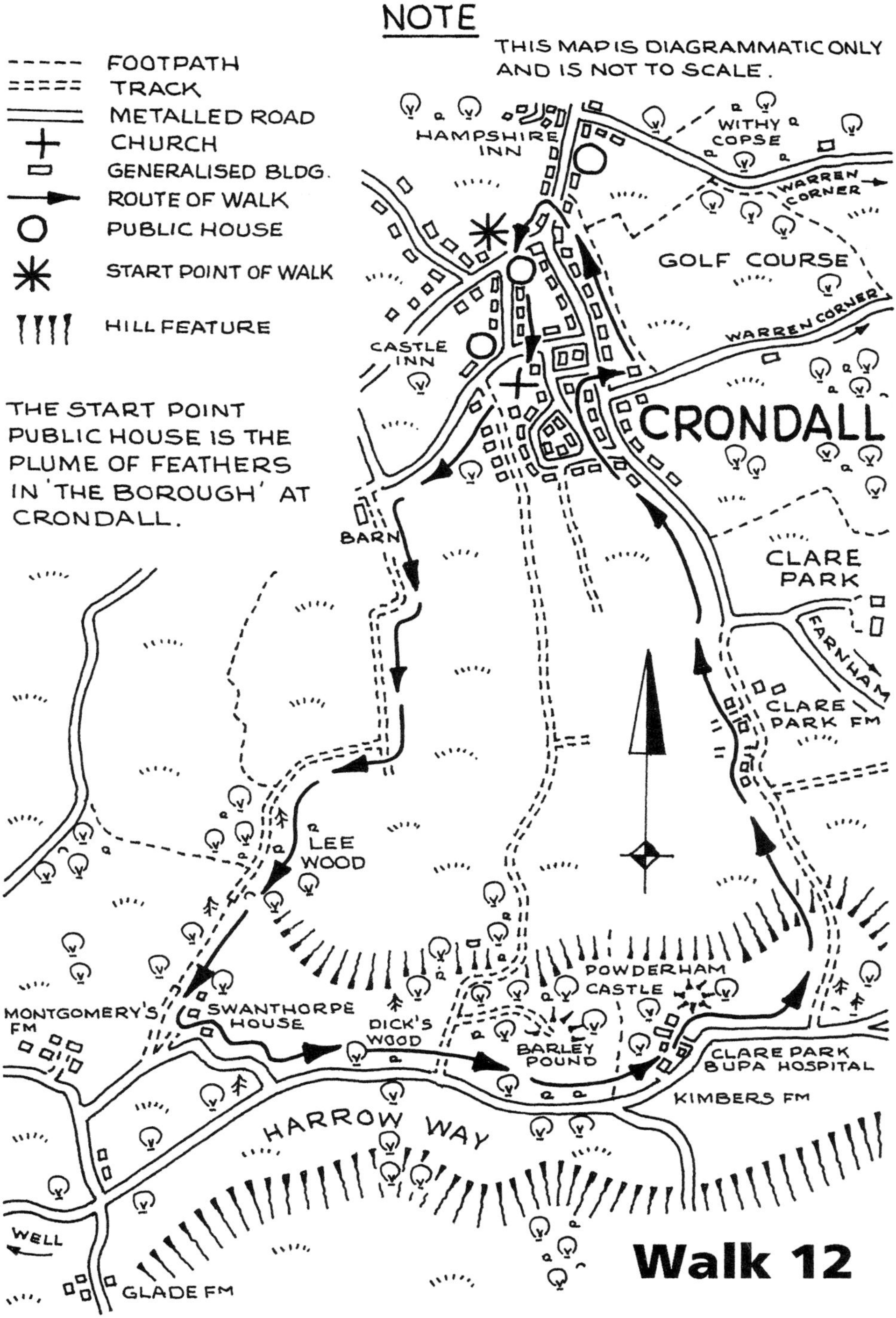

NOTE

THIS MAP IS DIAGRAMMATIC ONLY AND IS NOT TO SCALE.

FOOTPATH
TRACK
METALLED ROAD
CHURCH
GENERALISED BLDG.
ROUTE OF WALK
PUBLIC HOUSE
START POINT OF WALK
HILL FEATURE

THE START POINT PUBLIC HOUSE IS THE PLUME OF FEATHERS IN 'THE BOROUGH' AT CRONDALL.

HAMPSHIRE INN
WITHY COPSE
WARREN CORNER
GOLF COURSE
WARREN CORNER
CASTLE INN
CRONDALL
CLARE PARK
BARN
FARNHAM
CLARE PARK FM
LEE WOOD
POWDERHAM CASTLE
MONTGOMERY'S FM
SWANTHORPE HOUSE
DICK'S WOOD
BARLEY POUND
CLARE PARK BUPA HOSPITAL
KIMBERS FM
HARROW WAY
WELL
GLADE FM

Walk 12

ters of the outlaw and highwayman Adam de Gurdon. Continue
along the lane to a road fork, where
you swing left and briefly uphill
past Kimbers Farm and higher still
past the Clare Hospital. As the road
bears right at the top of the hill,
look to your left to a wood. Here,
lost in the trees, are the last relics of
Powderham Castle, once an ancient earthwork and then a Norman Castle. A little further on, just
before your lane divides, a track
leads off to the left. Take this and
pass a white metal gate on its right-
hand side and soon admire the
fine views from this exposed track
over towards Clare Park and
Bricksbury Hill to the north east.
In years to come, this view may be
denied as a belt of very young
saplings, now protected in tubes
from deer and rabbits, matures.

Crondall Church

Follow the track down towards the tile hung Windrush on your left and then past Clare Park Farm and Clare Park Farmhouse — the latter on your right with some fine topiary work in front and rear gardens. Soon you will arrive at the Crondall to Farnham road where you turn left. Care is needed at first, but soon there is a nice wide grass verge on the left for you to walk upon. Carry on, soon passing the Crondall village sign and crossing the road at Townsend Cottage to join the footway opposite. Proceed past the bus stop and The White House until you reach a road junction, where you turn right into a lane signed Ewshott and Golf Course. This is Heath Lane and as you walk along, look out for a house called Doules Head on your left. Shortly past this, turn left and pass to the left-hand side of a gate following the line of a little stream at the edge of the Crondall Golf Course. The path is quite well-defined and you cross two stiles to emerge on to Pankridge Street. Turn left and very soon you will be back at the Plume of Feathers.

Common lands and silver birch from Puttenham

WALK 13
Allow 2 ½ hours
4 ½ miles
Walk begins page 79

Background to the Walk

The village of Puttenham enjoys a sunny spot on the southern flank of that narrow chalk ridge called the Hogs Back. It is a pleasant village with many quaint brick cottages and in spite of chalklands being so near, I only saw flints used on one dwelling, which is surprising as there are many old chalk pits on the flanks of the Hogs Back. The main village street (called The Street) is dominated at its eastern end by the parish church of St John the Baptist standing high above the houses. The earliest part of the church is the south wall of the nave which is early Norman, circa 1100. The tower is 15th century but a fire, started in a blacksmith's forge nearby in 1735, destroyed the capping spire and most of the nave roof.

The church was not fully restored until 1861. At one time, a complex of buildings came right up to the church and one of these buildings had a well which was last used in 1750. When the buildings were removed, the well was filled in and forgotten until Palm Sunday 1972 when a cypress tree fell over to reveal the old well which was by now just inside the church gate. It has now been tidied up and a grill placed over its yawning depths.

Adjacent to the churchyard, and on the south side, is an impressive colour washed mansion known as Puttenham Priory. Formerly a stone building with brick gables, it was converted into the large square mansion with a Palladian style entrance we see today, by Thomas Parker in 1761. He also converted much of the surrounding land into a park. His predecessor at the Priory was General James Oglethorpe, who bought

Maps
Landranger 1:50,000
Sheet 186
Pathfinder 1:25,000
Sheet 1224 SU84/94
Map Reference of Start/
Finish SU931478

How to get there
From Farnham take A31 towards Guildford. On the Hogs Back look for the B3000 turn off left towards Godalming. Turn left to pass under A31 and proceed down the hill taking first right into Puttenham. The Good Intent is on your right past the church. From Camberley follow A325 to join A31 eastbound at the large roundabout east of Farnham and then proceed as above. Tillingbourne Bus Company run services 515 and 565 for shoppers through Puttenham from the Redgrave Theatre at Farnham but check with the bus company on 0483 276880 first. Stagecoach regular services 214 and 215 ply between Winchester and Guilford at hourly intervals via Farnham and the Hogs Back. If you alight at the Puttenham crossroads it is only a half mile walk off the Hogs Back down to Puttenham. From Camberley these services can be joined at Farnham by taking the regular

*through service F40
(Tillingbourne Bus Company)
at two-hourly intervals.*

Pub facilities
Good Intent,
Puttenham

*This charming village pub has
a central position in the village
of Puttenham opposite to the
Suffield lane junction. It is
white- and wide-fronted and
extends to the gabled annex
carrying the pub sign on the
left. Some parts of the building
date back to the 16th century
but its modern role is to cater
for locals, visitors and walkers
alike. Although the landlord is
tolerant of walker's boots, he
prefers rucksacks to be placed
out of the way. The bar area is
continuous throughout,
stretching from the pool table
area on the far left to the
inglenook fireplace in the
saloon area on your right. It is
a Courage house and provides
the range of their beers with
special ales such as the popular
Hogs Back, Ringwood and
Wadworth 6X plus a guest ale,
which changes frequently.
These, and other drinks, are
served from 11.00-14.30
and 18.00-23.00 (Mon-Fri), all
day Saturday and 12.00-
15.00,19.00-22.30 (Sun).
Enjoy food in this attractive,
red carpeted, low beamed pub
with a bar festooned overhead
with hop flowers. A menu and
daily specials board offered
calamares with a garlic dip,
steak sandwich with onions
and chips, battered seafood
platter and many other
tempting dishes when I called.
Prices are reasonable and there
is a dessert menu. Call in
between 12.00-14.00 every day
and 19.00-22.00 all evenings
except Sunday and Monday.*

The Good Intent at Puttenham

the mansion for £4,400 in 1745 but never lived there. He was MP for Haslemere and before purchasing the Priory, set sail for America in 1732 with 120 settlers founding the colony of Georgia before returning home and taking part in the routing of the Jacobites in the 1745-46 uprising.

Before the Second World War, there were many hop fields in the vicinity of the village with picking done by local families and itinerant workers who travelled about the hop fields of southern England. The hops used to be dried in the old hop kilns you will see on the left-hand side of The Street as you go up to the church. The kilns eventually became redundant but just recently they have been converted very tastefully into attractive residences, still retaining their oast house architecture.

The North Downs Way passes along the village street. This long distance footpath extends 153 miles from Farnham to Canterbury and Dover. It was formally opened in 1978 by the Archbishop of Canterbury, following 15 years of planning and negotiation. The Countryside Commission proposed that the route should follow closely the chalk ridge of the North Downs. You may find that, if you examine the Pathfinder map in grid square SU8947, the words North Downs Way (undefined) appear. This should be ignored as the full length of the path is now defined and waymarked. The responsibility of maintaining the path lies with the Surrey and Kent County Councils.

There is a special fish and chip night on Wednesdays between 18.00-21.30. Children and dogs are allowed in the bar and there is a small garden to the rear. The car park is also small, so ask permission if you wish to leave your car. It is entered by a narrow passage as the numerous scrape marks on the wall will testify, but it is passable with care proportional to the size of your car! There is parking on the street outside.
Tel 0483 810387.

Puttenham Church

Just over one mile to the south west of Puttenham, and strongly featured in this walk, is the territory of Bob Crompton, a genial, good-humoured Yorkshireman who acts as a Ranger for the Surrey County Council. His domain is the 470 acres of Puttenham Common, an area of silver birch, bracken and pine — a walkers' paradise crossed by numerous paths. It is typical Surrey heathland of Lower Greensand geology. Access is by agreement with the local landowner who resides in the nearby mansion of Hampton.

The same Thomas Parker who transformed Puttenham Priory purchased Hampton in 1766 and converted the existing house to a more classical style living there until he died in 1791. It was Thomas Parker who made the chain of attractive lakes which separate the Common from the parkland of Hampton. It is now the home of Richard Thornton, Lord Lieutenant of the County of Surrey and the imposing façade of the house may be glimpsed through the trees as you walk on the western side of the Common.

Walk 13

Distance: *Allow two-and-a-half hours for this walk of four-and-a-half miles*

Leave the pub and glance up to your right at the pub sign. The Good Intent has Civil war connections and depicted in the sign is a Roundhead soldier, kneeling with his helmet laid beside him and his sword upright in his hands. In the background are the tents of the Puritans' New Model Army. The 'God is on our side' belief pervades the minds of all combatants in war. Turn left and stroll up the lane to the church, passing on your left a fine modern conversion of oast houses to private residences. The church is well worth this short diversion at the beginning of the walk. Nave and chancel have 12th century origins while the north aisle was added 60 years later with north and south chapels provided in the 13th and 14th centuries respectively. Local artists have supplied pictures in various materials on the north aisle wall, showing the growth of the church. Outside in the churchyard, have a look at the adjacent Puttenham Priory brightly coloured in a buttermilk hue and possessing an impressive frontal colonnade.

After pausing to look at Puttenham's rediscovered well, retrace your steps down the lane and past the Good Intent. Pleasant brick cottages line your way up to the Post Office and general shop. Look for the Old Forge Cottage and Step Cottage (very appropriately named) before you take the left-hand fork at the Post Office named Lascombe Lane. A direction sign with an acorn logo reminds you that this is the North Downs Way. Shortly fork left again following Highfield Lane uphill past Carpenters Field on your right. Pause to take in the views on your left, where Puttenham Priory shows up very clearly and half left, where the dark wooded hills around Hindhead dominate the skyline, a sight viewed with some trepidation by former travellers on the old road to Portsmouth. The steep sunken lane leads past Lower Lascombe House to a more modern open section bordered on the left by ivy clad oaks. Look out for a footpath sign on your left pointing half right over arable land. Follow this well-defined path to a stile tucked away in trees and cross a meadow to a further stile. Cross a gravel access road and go straight forward to follow a fenced and hedged path to the right of a house. The path soon opens up and curves through woodland, arriving shortly at a wooden kissing gate with a glimpse of a house in trees to your left.

The kissing gate and accompanying fence form the eastern boundary of Puttenham Common, an area of bracken, pine and silver birch. Turn left on to the bridleway and then quickly right to follow a winding path, forking left when this soon divides. You now follow this path straight ahead ignoring all side paths, proceeding mainly downhill over the Common for well over half a mile to the car park by the Elstead road at the southern end of the Common. Half-way along this section, many paths converge and diverge in a woody dell and when emerging from this, take the main right-hand path up a short, sharp slope before your route resumes its downward trend again. Just after this, there is another major path junction and here take the route leading directly ahead.

The red soil you have encountered belongs to the Folkestone Beds of the Lower Greensand Series. It is loose and there are many signs of path erosion. Early man cleared the tree cover which resulted in a heathland landscape with low growing species such as heather and gorse. Order was maintained by grazing animals, but in the last hundred years this has practically ceased and invasive silver birch and bracken have become established. Efforts are being made to rejuvenate the heathland to encourage heather growth which is now virtually dormant and to clear the rampant bracken.

As you approach the car park, veer to the right of the short timber posts and head across the grass to pick up the path again at the far side of the picnic area. The Tarn glints in the trees to your right as you cross a stream and proceed uphill on a path swinging gradually right. You can deviate to the Tarn's edge if you wish. A fence

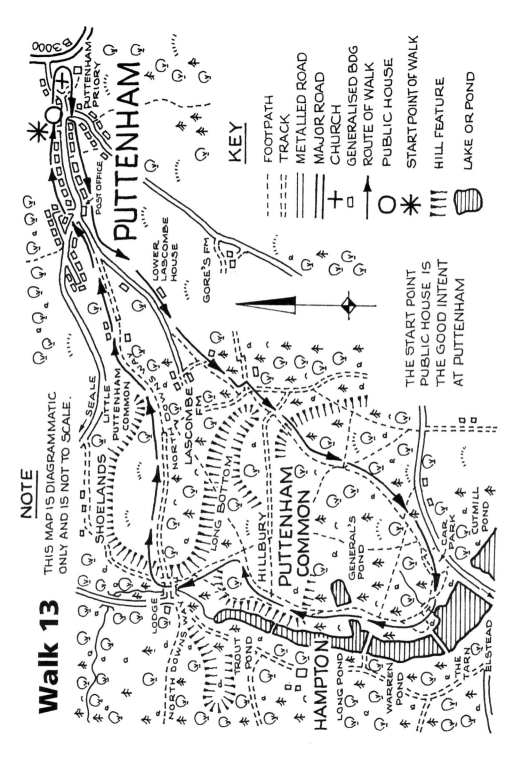

Walk 13

NOTE
THIS MAP IS DIAGRAMMATIC ONLY AND IS NOT TO SCALE.

KEY
- - - - FOOTPATH
= = = TRACK
===== METALLED ROAD
|||| MAJOR ROAD
✝ ☐ CHURCH
☐ GENERALISED BDG
➤ ROUTE OF WALK
O PUBLIC HOUSE
✳ START POINT OF WALK
ΛΛΛ HILL FEATURE
⬭ LAKE OR POND

THE START POINT PUBLIC HOUSE IS THE GOOD INTENT AT PUTTENHAM

B3000

PUTTENHAM

PUTTENHAM PRIORY

POST OFFICE

LOWER LASCOMBE HOUSE

GORE'S FM

SEALE

SHOELANDS

LITTLE PUTTENHAM COMMON

NORTH DOWN'S WAY

LASCOMBE FM

LODGE

LONG BOTTOM

HILLBURY

PUTTENHAM COMMON

GENERAL'S POND

CAR PARK

CUTMILL POND

HAMPTON

NORTH DOWNS WAY

TROUT POND

LONG POND

WARREN POND

THE TARN

ELSTEAD

appears on your left and your path keeps company with this, soon crossing a boardwalk and passing to the left of The General's Pond. This pond was used as a 'stew pond' to allow young carp to mature before being transferred to the main string of lakes. The pond was named after General Oglethorpe of Puttenham Priory. As you crossed the boardwalk you may have noticed the fine facade of Hampton House to your left.

Shortly after a muddy patch, fork right and climb steeply to Hillbury which was a pre-Roman fort but later used by the Romans.

Converted oast houses in Puttenham

Fine views are on offer in all directions, especially northwards to the Hogs Back. Follow the track straight over the summit and make your way down to a crossing of paths where you go left-handed, following the route through silver birch and bracken, keeping left at a fork in the path and left again at a T junction. At a further T junction, with a stream and a lodge to the Hampton Estate to your left, turn right to join the North Downs Way following this route back to the Good Intent. After climbing for some time, the path forks left leaving Puttenham Common and then a pleasant, undulating path borders Little Common to your left before the houses of Puttenham gradually enter your view and the path becomes a track and then finally a road.

Quiet waters and a lonely abbey from Runfold

WALK 14
Allow 3 ½ hours
5 ½ miles
Walk begins page 86

Background to the Walk

For many years, Runfold has been besieged by traffic pouring along the A31 between Farnham and Guildford but at last relief is imminent. Scheduled for completion in August 1994, the Runfold Diversion will take through traffic away from the houses and hopefully peace should return to this community which stretches from the Princess Royal pub to the start of the long climb to the summit of the Hogs Back.

Formerly a tithing of Farnham, Runfold never achieved the importance of some of its neighbours. The name itself means 'A place where trees have been felled' and even today, there is only a scattering of trees in the immediate locality. More prominent are the sand extraction pits stretching in an east-west line to the south of here — you will pass round the perimeter of one of these as you return from this walk. The current owners, Drinkwater Sabey, purchased the site in May 1991. Originally opened in 1951 by Ebenezer Mears, the sand workings are sited on the widest part of the Folkestone Beds which are particularly rich in sand for mortar, asphalt and concrete making processes. A quarter of a million tonnes are mined annually, most of this going to the London and South East areas, and even at this rate of extraction, the site has a life expectancy of another 20 years.

A little to the east of the Princess Royal pub lies Barfield School although the building has not always been a school. In 1895, John Henry Knight lived here and his passion was for engine driven vehicles. During that year he designed a two-seater car which was assembled by George Parfitt of the Elliot Reliance

Maps
Landranger 1:50,000
Sheet 186
Pathfinder 1:25,000
Sheet 1225 SU84/94
Map Reference of Start/
Finish SU863476

How to get there
From Farnham take A31
towards Guildford. Shortly
after the large roundabout east
of the town look for the
Princess Royal on your left.
From Camberley take A325 to
the roundabout mentioned
above and follow A31 left-
handed to the Princess Royal.
Stagecoach services 214 and
215 (Winchester - Farnham -
Guildford) go past the
Princess Royal on an hourly
basis. From Camberley,
Tillingbourne service F40
runs to Farnham on a 2-
hourly frequency to join the
above services.

***Pub facilities
Princess Royal,
Runfold***

This is a 1938-built road house named after Princess Mary, then the Princess Royal and is a large broad-fronted pub situated on the north side of A31 with a large, prominent conservatory adorning the road facing façade. The pub is spacious with a separate restaurant down steps to the left. The roomy conservatory provides plenty of seating space and light. The bar is carpeted throughout and has numerous archways leading to alcoves and seating areas. Opening times are between 11.00-14.30 with 17.30-23.00 in the evenings (Mon-Fri). 11.00-23.00 (Sat) and the normal 12.00-15.00 and 19.00-22.30 on Sundays. A large menu offers Mexican and traditional food ranging from enchilladas to steak and kidney pies. Jacket potatoes, salads, ploughmans and 3 types of vegetarian meals are available. There is a children's menu and 7 types of dessert. A roast Sunday lunch is always on offer. Food serving times are 12.00-14.15 and 17.30-22.00 (Mon-Fri), 12.00-14.45 and 17.30-22.00 (Sat) and 12.00-14.30 on Sundays. It is a free house but Courage ales feature prominently, together with Wadworth 6X, Websters, John Smiths, Beamish stout and lagers.Children are allowed anywhere in the pub and there is a garden with a play area. The present manager has run the pub for the last 15 years and is confident that the Runfold Diversion to the A31 will not affect his established trade (the new road will pass to the rear of the Princess

The Princess Royal at Runfold

Works in nearby Farnham. It was capable of 8 mph but had to be led by a man with a red flag at the stately speed of 4 mph. Like most of us, John Knight had moments of madness and on at least one occasion earned a speeding fine in the local court for exceeding this limit! He built many cars and tested them in the Runfold area.

South-west of Runfold is the valley of the River Wey (northern branch) and lying in this valley at Compton Bridge, is Moor Park House which you pass on the walk. I am sure you will admire its arched gatehouse surmounted by a clock with a cupola-topped round tower on the left side. This is the Campana Finishing School for girls from 16 years upwards which offers courses including Cordon Bleu cookery, Etiquette and Musical Appreciation in addition to more academic studies. The building also houses the Constance Spry Flower School. Constance Spry designed flower arrangements for many Royal occasions, including the Queen's coronation in 1953. The main house is Georgian but there has been a building here since the 16th

Royal). The car park is large and walkers are welcome to leave their cars with permission. A feature of the pub is the large collection of old John Player's and WD & HO Wills cigarette cards with footballers, cricketers, servicemen and Royalty adorning the walls. Tel 0252 782243.

Left: Waverley Abbey — a romantic ruin

century. Sir William Temple, a well-known diplomat and essayist of his time, bought the house about 1680 and employed Jonathan Swift of *Gulliver's Travels* fame as private secretary for ten years.

Waverley Abbey, built in 1128, now lies in ruins but is featured in this walk and merits special attention. Little remains of this once fine Abbey on the banks of the Wey — the first of the Cistercian Order to be founded in this country. Originating from the Abbey of Citeaux in Normandy, the Cistercians were a simple and austere order whose buildings were devoid of decoration. Their cloth habits were of undyed wool and hence they were nicknamed the White Monks. Twelve Cistercians arrived from the Abbey of Aumone in France with their Abbott, John, for the foundation ceremony on 24 November 1128 by William Gifford, Bishop of Winchester. After troubles during the reign of King John, who forbade any movement of Cistercians, the Abbey prospered until the Dissolution when the destructive hand of Henry's henchman, Thomas Cromwell, fell heavily upon Waverley. Further deprivations reduced the Abbey to the few relics you see now. There are guided tours at weekends (Tel 0252 783579).

Benefiting from the building stone taken from the Abbey, is Waverley Abbey House looking out from its dominating position beyond the lake to the Abbey ruins. Chancellor of the Exchequer John Aislabie built the house in 1723 which eventually passed to George Nicholson, brother-in-law of Florence Nightingale, a frequent visitor, as was Sir Walter Scott who took inspiration for the *Waverley Novels* from the surroundings. The house is now owned by the Crusade for World Revival and is called the Waverley Christian Training Centre. It is an interdenominational Christian Charity and trains students from all over the world.

From the Wey Valley there is a climb to the heights of Crooksbury Hill, a dominant, pine-clad summit, 535ft above sea level. The views are extensive and well worth the climb. Shortly after descending, you walk along a small part of the 153-mile-long North Downs Way.

Walk 14

Distance: *Allow three-and-a-half hours for this walk of five-and-a-half miles*

On leaving the Princess Royal, turn right and cross the busy road with care, passing the bus stop to enter an access road on the left and soon turning left on a gravel track by a public bridleway sign. Follow this, keeping straight ahead where the track bends left and pass through the farm buildings of Kilnside Farm. The Wey Valley opens up ahead as you arrive at a track junction with Wey Cottage on your left. Turn left here and continue past two attractive cottages, strikingly different in architectural style. Beyond these cottages, the road becomes metalled and the River Wey (Northern Branch) comes in closer on your right. Shortly, this road meets Compton Way and as we approached the road junction, an archery contest was taking place in the riverside meadows to the right. Cross directly over Compton Way to a small gate on the left-hand side of metal gates and enter the precincts of Moor Park House. Carry on with the interesting school buildings on your right (note the archway surmounted by a clock with the date 1890 to the right of a turret). The main white house is listed as a building of historic interest and stands further along on your right.

Cross a stile alongside a wooden gate and continue along a pleasant valley path with the river on the right and a wooded bank on the left for well over half a mile. On the way you will see fine parkland trees, a ruined building, two old brick pill boxes and Mother Ludlam's cave, who was by local legend, a white or benign witch. I hope she found her sandstone cave to be homely and comfortable! At the end of this long path you arrive on Camp Hill via the pea gravel driveway of Stella Lodge.

If you would like to visit the ruins of Waverley Abbey, turn right on B3001 as you reach Camp Hill, crossing the Wey at Waverley Bridge and veer left by South Lodge, leaving the entrance to Waverley Abbey House on your right. Pass through a wooden kissing gate to the left of a metal gate and go ahead on a curving gravel track with a lake on your right and lush meadowland on your left. The grand façade and lawns of Waverley Abbey House come into view on your right well before you reach a stile and a metal pedestrian gate. Move into the meadow beyond by using either of these and follow the field path to a kissing gate adjacent to a wooden farm gate. You now enter the grounds of Waverley Abbey. Not much remains of this first Cistercian Abbey, but what does is interpreted on small plaques attached to the stonework.

Retrace your steps back over the Wey to where B3001 turns sharply right at the junction with Camp Hill and follow it uphill for about a quarter mile taking care around a left-hand bend. Look out for the brick walled entrance to Keepers Cottage and take a left turning track at the far end of the wall. Follow this curving track past Yew Tree and other cottages until you reach a road where you turn left uphill and follow the road over a crest. Just beyond the crest turn right on to a track leading into Crooksbury Hill car park, which is oval in shape with two central islands. Take a path leading off at eleven o'clock and climb up through silver birch

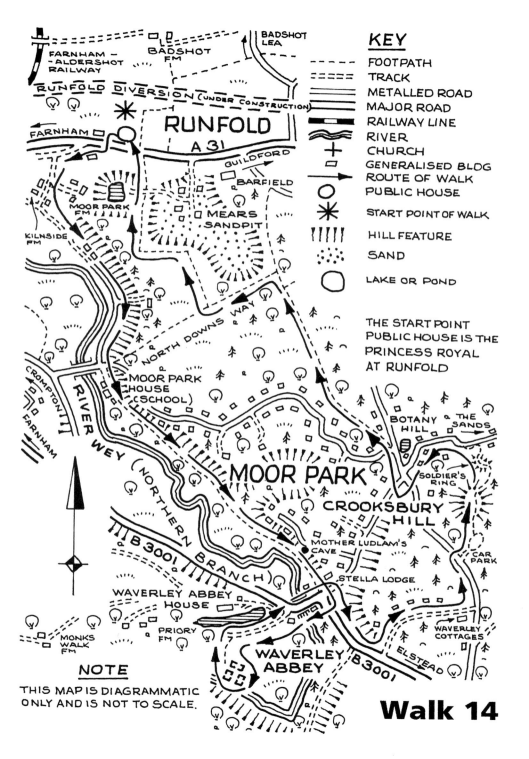

KEY

FOOTPATH
TRACK
METALLED ROAD
MAJOR ROAD
RAILWAY LINE
RIVER
CHURCH
GENERALISED BLDG
ROUTE OF WALK
PUBLIC HOUSE
START POINT OF WALK

HILL FEATURE

SAND

LAKE OR POND

THE START POINT
PUBLIC HOUSE IS THE
PRINCESS ROYAL
AT RUNFOLD

Walk 14

NOTE

THIS MAP IS DIAGRAMMATIC
ONLY AND IS NOT TO SCALE.

woodland, reaching steps as the path steepens. After toiling up the steps, your efforts are rewarded by the sight of a white Ordnance Survey trig pillar with a plinth that affords a resting place while you enjoy the view to the south. The pillar was restored in 1991 as part of the OS bi-centenary celebrations and in recognition of the services of Theodore Durrant, Surrey Planning Officer from 1951 to 1968.

After your rest, proceed directly ahead and begin to descend through pines. At a fork, take the right-hand path and then shortly fork left, descending to a bridleway where you turn left. Turn right almost immediately where a sign says no horses and keep to the right as the path forks straight away. You soon pass through Soldiers Ring, an ancient earthwork amid the pines. Cross the ramparts and go down a steep bank taking the right-hand path at the base, soon meeting a bridleway by a blue marker post.

Riverside cottages by the Wey

Turn left here, following the path to descend to a small car park with a road beyond. Turn left on to the road and proceed uphill and then eventually downhill past fine houses to a road junction. Bear right and arrive at the junction with Compton Way on your left. Turn half left between the two roads to a path indicated by a public bridleway sign, following this pleasant pathway behind the substantial houses of Moor Park for nearly half a mile. Ignore a foot path sign on the left before joining the North Downs Way which arrives from the right.

At a sign post which was damaged as we passed, follow the North Downs Way and turn left up wooden steps and over a low stile. Continue along a fenced path with oak and beech on either side and after passing through a group of horse chestnuts, cross a wooden stile and carry on with a barbed wire fence to your right. Look out for a stile on your right where we found another broken footpath sign. Cross the stile and head downhill with a wire fence on your left, admiring the northerly views as you go. Soon your path is fenced on each side as you are firmly guided around the western perimeter of a sand extraction site and you route is unmistakable as you descend concrete steps, cross a works track and rise again by similar steps until you meet the A31 again after crossing a stile. Descend steps and cross the main road with extreme care back to the pub car park.

Downland hills and a village pond from Well

WALK 15
Allow 4 hours
6 miles
Walk begins page 91

Background to the Walk

The hamlet of Well lies in true Hampshire downland with the twin hills of Horsedown Common to the north and with high, wooded downland to the south. It is a pretty collection of farms and cottages astride the ancient Harrow Way which stretches across the South Country from the Cornish tin mines to London and the Kentish ports. The name Well simply means a place at the spring or stream and you can see a reedy pond near the crossroads above the Chequers Inn. The actual well itself lies on the opposite side of the lane and has a concrete capping over a brick shaft. A wood-framed canopy with a tiled roof, surmounted by a wooden Saxon style cross, shields it from the weather. William Fullerton, who lived at Well Manor, gave the well to the hamlet before he died in 1888, but the well is ancient and was in existence a long time before it became a gift. The canopy was placed over the shaft to celebrate Queen Victoria's Silver Jubilee in 1862 and nearly 100 years later it was extensively renovated on the occasion of the Festival of Britain in 1951.

Well does not have its own parish and instead it falls within the boundaries of the parish of Long Sutton, a village over a mile away to the west. Like Well, Long Sutton also straddles the Harrow Way and it is said that pilgrims making for Canterbury stopped for refreshments at the 13th century church of All Saints in Long Sutton. A south chapel was added to the church for the benefit of passing pilgrims and was known as the pilgrims' chapel. In medieval times the village was known as Sheep Sutton which indicates the type of farming carried on in these parts. Many shepherds and

Maps
Landranger 1:50,000
Sheet 186
Pathfinder 1:25,000
Sheet 1224 SU64/74
Map Reference of Start/
Finish SU761466

How to get there
From Farnham take A325
West Street and turn right up
Crondall Lane. Look for the
turning left for Dippenhall
and take the second left
turning after that (signed
Long Sutton) past Clare Park
Hospital for 3 miles to the
hamlet of Well. You will find
the Chequers on your right
just past Well cross roads.
From Camberley join M3 and
proceed to junction 5 where
you follow A287 left-handed
as far as the roundabout. Here
take B3349 and pass through
North Warnborough and the
western part of Odiham. Look
for Odiham Airfield on your
left and descend to a cross
roads where you turn left
towards Long Sutton. Pass
through the village and one-
and-a-half miles further on is
the hamlet of Well with the
Chequers on your left. It is not
possible to reach Well by
public transport but you can
get to LongSutton and begin
the walk there. Hampshire Bus
service 210 runs infrequently
from Alton to Basingstoke via

Long Sutton. Hampshire Bus
service 214 and 215 run
between Farnham and Alton
to connect with service 210.
From Camberley service 200
runs to Basingstoke and you
can connect with service 210
if you alight at the Hatch
public house. Do not attempt
the journey before checking
with the company on 0256
464501.

Pub facilities
Chequers,
Well
Standing alongside the
ancient Harrow Way, there
has been an inn on the site of
the Chequers for hundreds of
years. The present building
dates from 1540 and there is a
record of an inn before that.
Adjacent cottages used to
serve as stables in the days
when the Harrow Way was a
busy route. The present
landlord took over the pub 4
years ago and has maintained
it in the tradition of a wayside
inn. He is a local man and has
never lived more than 3 miles
from The Chequers. The
entrance is through the open-
fronted, vine festooned Vinery
with long tables and benches
which are very popular in the
summer. There are three inter-
connected bar areas placed on
different levels where you can
order Boddingtons or
Wethereds special ales
together with Flowers
Original Bitter. Those who
prefer lager are catered for by
Stella Artois or Heineken all
obtainable between the hours
of 11.00-15.00 and 17.30-
23.00 (Mon-Sat) or12.00-
15.00 and 19.00-22.30 on
Sunday. Bar food is displayed
on a blackboard and together
with the restaurant food, is

The Chequers at Well — on the ancient Harrow Way

their flocks would have passed along Harrow Way to
and from local markets.

The church, which you pass on the walk, is built of
flint and rubble with stone quoins and in the nave of the
church you can see the four massive oak pillars which
support the 15th Century bell tower. The tremendous
load bearing resulted in major repairs being necessary
between 1947 and 1959 when old timbers were replaced by steel girders. If you wish to see something
really ancient, step into the churchyard at the rear of the
church where you will see a truly venerable yew tree.
Stand inside its shattered and gnarled trunk and try to
imagine what Long Sutton and the surrounding countryside looked like when the yew was a mere sapling.
There are two more yews, only slightly younger, at the
front of the church adjacent to the road. Around the
corner of the lane which you follow past the church is
the village pond — a credit to the village. Well trimmed
grass and a sylvan background makes this a compel-
ling spot to pause, rest awhile and admire.

Between Well and Long Sutton is the Lord Wandsworth College, set in 1,200 acres of farmland. Sydney
James Stern was born in 1844, of wealthy parents and
he eventually inherited a considerable fortune from
banking and finance. He became interested in politics
and in 1891 became the liberal MP for Stowmarket in

Suffolk, becoming the author of a parliamentary bill for the better housing of the working classes in rural districts. In 1895 he was elevated to the Peerage partly because of his generous donations to Party funds. He selected the title of Lord Wandsworth as he owned a good deal of property in the London borough. He died in 1912 and as he never married, his title died with him. The greater part of his considerable fortune was left to charitable causes, one of which was the foundation of a residential institution for children. This manifested itself in 1914 with the purchase of two farms in the Long Sutton area and the establishment of an orphanage. This is how the Lord Wandsworth College originated and gradually it has developed into the spacious complex of buildings we see today, although the original orphan concept was quickly diluted by children who had a single parent. Fee paying pupils were accepted in 1945 and now comprise 75% of the total of over 400 pupils who attend the college as boarders. Old boys formed the Old Sternians Association in 1950 and this group is still thriving.

famed for miles around. If you fancy smoked salmon with scrambled eggs, or Malaysian lamb curry with rice, or even a bacon and avocado baguette, this is the place for you. There are starters and desserts all available between 12.00-14.30 and 19.00-22.00 (Mon-Sat), 12.00-14.30 and 19.00-21.30 on Sunday. There is a charmimg restaurant which seats 16. It has a separate menu but is not open on Sundays and Mondays. To the rear of the pub is a large garden with upturned barrels acting as tables. There are no childrens amusements. Walkers may leave their cars in the car park with permission. Tel 0256 862605.

Walk 15

Distance: *Allow four hours for this walk of six miles*

As you leave the vinery of The Chequers, bear left along the lane running past the pub car park, shortly arriving at a T junction opposite a square-fronted brick house with a large inset giving the date 1686. Turn right up a rise and pass the hamlet's well, wooden framed with a tiled roof and a wooden Saxon-style cross on top. Proceed over the cross roads with Manor Farm on your left. In 200 yards, turn right off the lane to join a track indicated by a Right of Way sign. This is Frog Lane and you follow this sunken route beneath oak and beech, the air being heavy with the scent of cow parsley when we passed. Views of Lord Wandsworth College open up on your right before you head back into the trees briefly and a fine vista of open downland countryside soon unfolds. Alongside hedgerows of field maple, ash, hazel, elder and hawthorn, continue up the valley, swinging right to follow the track through a small clump of sycamores.

Shortly you join a metalled road from a wisteria-clad part of the college on your right and proceed down to a T-junction of metalled access roads. Cross a stile directly opposite and take a half-left route across arable land to a visible stile on the far boundary. This path was clearly defined when we used it. On joining a lane, turn right and pass Hyde Farm, which is another part of Lord Wandsworth College, noticing the brick-arched access surmounted by a clock showing a seemingly permanent two-minutes-to-ten. This again is topped by a cupola and

Well, well the Well at Well!

a weather vane cock. Continue along a road past estate cottages, college buildings dated 1928 and Long Sutton village school, finally emerging onto the Long Sutton to Well road. Here, turn left to enter the village and soon you will see the Church of All Saints on the right. Spare time to enter the churchyard and admire the three ancient yew trees, two at the front and a primeval-looking, hollow veteran at the rear. Spare time also to look around this plain but interesting church.

Continue now along the road and as you turn a right-hand corner, the pride of Long Sutton will delight you in the shape of the village pond with its tenants of moorhen, mallard and domestic duck. It has a sylvan background enhanced by a fine copper beech. Sit down awhile on the seat provided and enjoy the tranquillity. Eventually tear yourself away and join the lane opposite called Copse Lane and proceed away from the pond. There are some fine cottages on view, including The Old Granary on your right. Follow this lane for three-quarters of a mile with verges alive with bluebells, stitchwort, cow parsley, campion, speedwell, vetch and a sprinkling of dandelions. How verdant and beautiful the countryside looked on this Spring day! Where the lane turns sharply right at a cluster of houses and a rear entrance to Lord Wandsworth College, take a track directly ahead indicated by a footpath sign. Where the track bends right and peters out in an arable field go through the gap into the field and turn left (a waymark arrow indicates the route). Carry on by the left-hand side of this large field along a defined path under

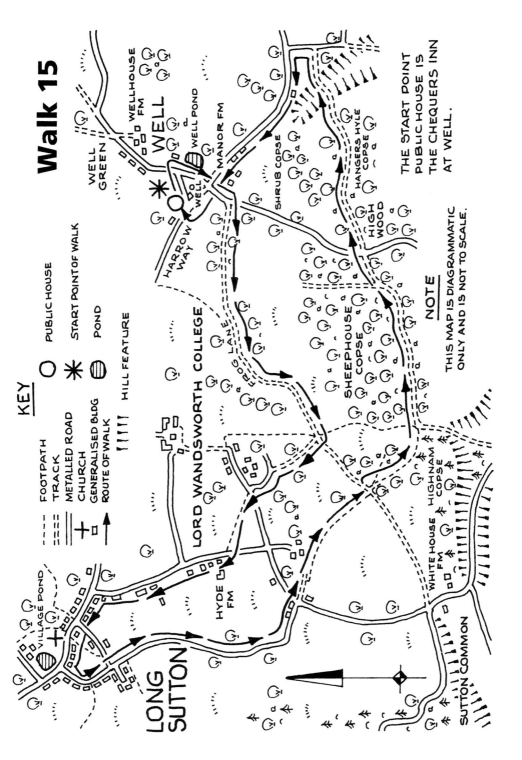

Walk 15

KEY

O PUBLIC HOUSE

✳ START POINT OF WALK

▨ POND

- - - - FOOTPATH
≡≡≡≡ TRACK
══════ METALLED ROAD
✝ CHURCH
▯ GENERALISED BLDG
↑ ROUTE OF WALK

▥ HILL FEATURE

THE START POINT
PUBLIC HOUSE IS
THE CHEQUERS INN
AT WELL.

NOTE

THIS MAP IS DIAGRAMMATIC
ONLY AND IS NOT TO SCALE.

WELL GREEN

WELLHOUSE FM

WELL

WELL POND

MANOR FM

SHRUB COPSE

HANGERS HYLE COPSE

HIGH WOOD

SHEEPHOUSE COPSE

HIGHNAM COPSE

WHITE HOUSE FM

SUTTON COMMON

HARROW WAY

LORD WANDSWORTH COLLEGE

CROSS LANE

HYDE FM

LONG SUTTON

VILLAGE POND

transmission lines to join a track after passing over a stile. You will enjoy the ever-expanding views along this section.

Turn left and then immediately right to join another track, ignoring an inviting path through the trees on the left which quickly forks from your route. You have now entered Sheephouse Copse which will be your companion for over half a mile. Oak, hazel and beech will shade your track which bends hard left at a field corner and a short diversion soon avoids a muddy area as your track becomes more like a path. A field soon appears on your left with mixed woodland on your right followed by a track joining from the right and a path from the left. Continue on the track straight ahead which contains another diversion (a fairly long one this time) to avoid a lengthy muddy area, before you arrive at a small clearing. Ignore a path heading deep into woodland on your left and follow the track down to the right. A watery depression soon appears on your left which is a seasonal pond, dry but yielding as we investigated. Pass by a metal barrier on to Well Lane where you turn left and then immediately right to join another track. Your route now takes you along the northern fringes of at first High Wood and then Hangers Hyle Copse with beech, oak, hazel and some ash. Ignore a path which branches right and carry on, following the track which veers slightly left, eventually leading through a muddy area to join a more pronounced track coming in from the right.

The light green foliage of beech is a delight in Spring and together with a carpet of bluebells, makes an idyllic combination. Your track now descends and then ascends to join a narrow lane where you turn left and eventually reach the top of the ridge. Here you meet the now-metalled Harrow Way and turn left, where you proceed downhill past a cottage on your left then rising under transmission lines to Manor Farm at Well and then over the cross roads to The Chequers on your right.

River valley and pine lands from Tilford

WALK 16
Allow 3 hours
5 miles
Walk begins page 97

Background to the Walk

The village of Tilford nestles in a valley where the two branches of the River Wey unite, the northern branch rising in the chalklands near Alton while the southern branch gathers itself in the many wooded ravines to the south of Hindhead. The northern arm has always been known as the River Wey but its southern counterpart has been called the River Till or the Tilford River in the past, hence the name Tilford from the Saxon word 'Til' meaning good or useful. So we have a 'useful ford'. The village is well known for its two fine mediaeval bridges, both 500 years old. The easterly bridge spanning the Wey where a ford used to be and the westerly one crossing the southern branch of the river.

The pride and joy of Tilford is its green, given to the village in 1853 by the Manor of Farnham for recreational purposes. The grass was neat and well trimmed when we visited with the hallowed cricket pitch occupying a central position. It was here that 'Silver Billy' Beldham wielded a lusty bat many years ago, as a cricket prodigy whose fame lives on in the village. He was born at nearby Wrecclesham in 1766 and came from farming stock by birth and in his attitude to our summer game. He played cricket for the famous Hambledon Club in Hampshire and his last big game was for the Players against the Gentlemen at Lords in 1821. He moved to Tilford in 1820 and played many matches on the green. He is once said to have hit a six which cleared both the Tilford Oak and the River Wey. After a spell as landlord of the Barley Mow, overlooking the green, he ended his days in Oak Cottage near the huge Tilford Oak, dying at the age of 96 in 1862.

Maps
Landranger 1:50,000
Sheet 186
Pathfinder 1:25,000
Sheet 1225 SU84/94
Map Reference of Start/
Finish
SU873434

How to get there
From Farnham cross A31 at the traffic lights and proceed on B3001 taking the right fork signed Tilford at the railway station. Follow this signed road for two-and-a-half miles to Tilford. As you cross the river bridge turn left at the corner of the green to arrive at the Barley Mow on your left. From Camberley follow A325 to the large roundabout east of Farnham. Turn right to follow A31 westbound to the traffic lights and take B3001 to the left. Then follow the above instructions to arrive at the Barley Mow. The restricted Stagecoach service 517 runs from Farnham to Hindhead via Tilford, designed to serve shoppers on Tuesdays and Fridays only. Alternatively walkers could use Stagecoach services 219 or 519 from Farnham and alight at The Mariners at Frensham, walking over the river bridge and taking the left turning lane signposted Frensham Little Pond and walking just

over one mile to join the walk where it meets Grange Road.

Pub facilities
Barley Mow
Tilford
Looking out over the village green, the Barley Mow has been a pub for 200 years and offers its customers two bars and a restaurant. Both bars have fireplaces while the restaurant has a stove. The restaurant is an attractive feature of the pub and is called The Beldham Bar in memory of 'Silver Billy' Beldham of local fame. Children are not allowed in the bars but are welcome in the restaurant while Wellington boots are not welcome in the Village Bar to the left of the front entrance (no not even green wellies says the notice!) The Barley Mow is a Courage house but guest ales are also on offer including Ringwood 49 and Wadworth 6X. A full range of Courage beers are supported by John Smiths', Beamish Irish stout, LA lager, Kronenberg and Fosters. The food is good with many tempting dishes including Penny's home made steak and kidney pie, fisherman's pie, home cured ham and jumbo pork sausages, scampi, sirloin or gammon steaks with at least two vegetarian meals and many other dishes together with a specials board. There are cream teas with home made cakes between 14.00- 18.00 on Saturdays, Sundays and Bank Holidays from Easter to the end of August. Pub opening times during the week are 11.00-14.30 and 18.00-23.00, with 11.00-15.00 and 18.00-23.00 Saturdays. Sunday opening times are the

The Barley Mow at Tilford

Mention of the Tilford Oak requires me to say a few words about this venerable tree at the north west corner of the green. William Cobbett in his *Rural Rides* stated that it was "the finest tree I ever saw in my life". He viewed it with awe while accompanied by his son James. It has a girth of 26ft and is reckoned to be 350 years old, but Cobbett would be sad to see it now. The tree has been doctored and a rather unsightly sheath has been placed to protect a damaged part of the bole.

Tilford acquired the status of a village and parish relatively recently as it was only in July 1867 that the village church was consecrated. It lies to the south of the green on the right hand side of the Rushmoor road as you go up the hill. The foundation stone was laid in July 1866 so construction work on this spacious church was very speedily completed. It is built of local sandstone and has a wide nave with an aisle on the south side. A plaque commemorates Harold Martin Soames, a lieutenant of the 20th Hussars killed at Binche near Mons on Sunday 23 August 1914. He was on patrol duty and was one of the first, if not the first British soldier killed in that holocaust.

Much of this walk is across the sandy wastelands of Hankley Common which is particularly arid in parts. Pine, silver birch, heather, bracken and gorse dominate and in such an environment, it is not surprising that

normal 12.00-15.00 and 19.00-22.30. Food serving times are 12.00-14.00 seven days a week and 19.00-21.00 each day except Sundays. There are summer barbecues in the garden at the rear and you can watch cricket on the village green sitting out in front of the pub at weekends. Tel 0252 2205.

Tilford Church

reptiles thrive. The rare sand lizard and the smooth snake are at home here but you will be lucky if you see either of these creatures. At the northern end of the Common lies Stockbridge Pond which was formed artificially to replace the earlier Abbott's Pond situated further upstream originally supplying the monks of Waverley Abbey with fish. Unfortunately Abbotts Pond burst in 1841 and was never restored.

Although this is not traditional socialist territory, a Labour Minister spent the last few years of his life in these parts. He was Philip Snowden, Chancellor of the Exchequer in the pre-war Labour and then National governments. Together with Ramsey Macdonald, he built up the Labour Party from small beginnings. The literary and architectural fields are also represented in the form of J. M. Barrie who penned *Peter Pan* at Black Lake Cottage about a mile to the north west of Tilford and Sir Edwin Lutyens, who designed the Tilford Institute on the west side of the green and much else of note around the country, and also lived locally.

Walk 16

Distance: *Allow three hours for this walk of five miles*

On leaving the Barley Mow cross over to the beautifully kept village green and savour your surroundings. To your right over the river as you face the pub lies the main village with shops and post office. Also on that side is the early 17th Century Bridge Farm, timber framed with brick infill. To the left of the Barley Mow is the ancient Tilford Oak with Oak Cottage on its nearside. Over to the west side of the green is the black and white village Institute with its centrally mounted clock designed by Sir Edwin Lutyens who lived nearby and completed in 1893.

From here walk along the road past the Tilford oak to the road junction on the north west corner of the green. Cross the road here and pass through an open gate flanked by a footpath sign on the left. Veer left towards a nursery and immediately fork right where you see a footpath sign obviously erected by the owners of the Nursery to guide walkers. Follow this hedge flanked path bending left and giving views of the River Wey (southern branch) on your right. Pass through a gate and enter deciduous woodland with the river still on your right. A rustic log seat gives a particularly fine view of the tree framed river.

Your path now veers away from the water and continues on a wooded course until you meet a track which you follow right handed past two houses on the right. As the track veers left towards an implement shed take the path going ahead through pines which give way to silver birch where we saw several pigs rooting happily among the trees. A very low stile precedes a track where you turn right.

You are now seeing a transition from the alluvial lands adjacent to the banks of the River Wey supporting deciduous woodland, to the native Greensand soils giving a heathland aspect to the landscape, supporting pines, silver birch and bracken. Follow the fenced track for a little way until another track leads off to the left opposite a gate. This track leads directly to another gate and your path passes to the left of this. With pines on the left and a deer fence on the right you pass through an area where coniferous seedlings are being nurtured to provide future planting, the younger ones being covered by plastic sheeting. Follow this path over an access track and presently swing right to reach Grange Road which you follow left handed until you reach and cross the Tilford to Hindhead road. Continue along a short length of concrete roadway past a small car park to your right and over a stream. You now enter Hankley Common proceeding directly ahead, ignoring right and left turning paths. You have two warnings in a short distance, firstly this is a military training area and you are warned of sudden noises and movements, while further on you are asked to be aware of the danger from flying golf balls! With ears and eyes suitably alert, cross over a track and go straight ahead, ignoring a path branching right. The golf course is on your left with the verdant fairways and greens contrasting sharply with the heathland. Follow the track towards a low pine clad ridge and ignore all side paths. The sandy track splits and joins again with another sign in the centre of the split warning that this is an Army training area and you are advised not to touch any suspicious objects.

At the top of the incline cross over another track, after noting on the right the remains of a substantial reinforced concrete wall, probably used by the military for training purposes. This area is marked on the OS map as The Lion's Mouth but we saw no obvious explanation for this nomenclature and no big cats! Where the path forks by a bridleway post, take the left hand path gradually descending through silver birch and pine to another fork with a bridleway sign. Take the right hand path this time and carry on over a stream to a junction of paths. Take the track leading half left and follow this through pines, ignoring all side paths until the pines give way to an open, particularly arid looking area. At a bridleway sign, turn left on a gravel track towards a pine capped knoll. Follow the track over the knoll pausing to take in the view over a very desolate extent of Hankley Common.

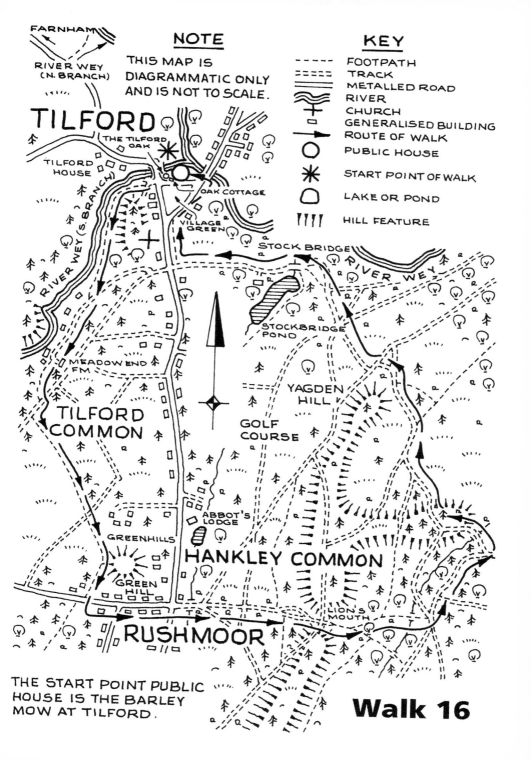

Walk 16

Bridge over the River Wey

Descend to where the track curves gently right at the bottom, receiving two tracks from the left. Take the main sandy track where a lesser track veers right and cross the low shoulder of Yagdon Hill which rises to your left and carry on until you reach a fork where you go left. Turn left again and then almost immediately right heading through extensive heather to where six paths meet. You route lies directly ahead towards a pine wood which you enter and at a scissors junction of paths keep left down a sunken track veering right and joining a track from the right before passing over a stream.

Stockbridge Pond lies to your left, a peaceful haven for local fishermen. Your track curves away right-handed past the wrought iron gates of Hankley Edge to your left and the welcome sight of green meadowland on your right. A car park on your left precedes the junction of your track with the Tilford to Hindhead road. Do not enter the road but pass through a green gate on your right to follow a path parallel to the road dedicated to pedestrians and equestrians. This leads downhill to the green and your car. If you wish to visit the 19th century church, it lies on your left as you pass through the path exit gate.

Footbridges, streams and ponds from Frensham

WALK 17
At least 3 hours
5 miles
Walk begins page 103

Background to the Walk

The village of Frensham lies in the valley of the River Wey (southern branch) some three miles south of Farnham, the majority of dwellings clustered near the Parish church of St. Mary the Virgin, lying west of the main Farnham to Hindhead road. South-west of the village is Frensham Manor, passed on this walk but not in view. Formerly known as Frensham Beale, after a family of that name, it is now a farmhouse built mainly of local sandstone. The old family name is commemorated in Bealeswood Common to the west. The manor passed from the Beale family in 1583 and in more modern times was acquired by Richard Combe from nearby Pierrepont in 1888 who was a member of the Watney, Combe and Reid brewing concern. It is now owned by the Powell family.

Frensham, originally Fermesham in the 10th Century means 'the homestead or village of a man called Fremi' but there is no record of who he was. Passers-by may be under the impression that Frensham is the substantial collection of houses on the north bank of the Wey where The Mariners is located. This is not so as the area is known as Millbridge which may in fact be a misnomer because there is no record of a mill being here. Frensham Mill is situated upstream near Frensham Manor and you will pass through the courtyard of the mill on this walk. Opposite the Mariners pub you will see the gates of Pierrepont, a rather grand sounding name for a school, but then it has not always been a school. The house was built in the mid-18th Century and shortly after this, the Duke of Kingston took it over and enlarged it, calling the house Pierrepont Lodge

Maps
Landranger 1:50,000
Sheet 186
Pathfinder 1:25,000
Sheet 1225 SU84/94
Map Reference of Start/
Finish SU848421

How to get there
From Farnham, follow the signing for A287 Hindhead and continue for two-and-a-half miles to Millbridge. The Mariners is situated to your right immediately preceding the bridge over the River Wey. From Camberley, follow the A325 southbound until you meet A31 at the large roundabout east of Farnham. Turn right here and follow A31 westwards to the traffic lights where you turn left and follow the signing for A287 Hindhead then proceed as above to The Mariners. The 219 and 519 Stagecoach bus services run between Aldershot and Haslemere via Farnham and Frensham with a bus stop outside The Mariners. The frequency is about one bus per hour and there is also a Stagecoach Sunday service 507 from Farnham and back via Dockenfield and Frensham. To join these services from Camberley take the Tillingbourne Bus Company service F40 through to Farnham.

Pub facilities
Mariners Inn, Frensham

This gabled pub has been extended into an hotel and is in prime position on the Farnham to Hindhead road (A287). It has a historical background of contraband and smuggling, an Italian proprietor and a fine maritime-flavoured restaurant with draped fishing nets, crab baskets, a frozen heron, a tiled floor and a fine mural of the French fishing port of Honfleur. The bar is U-shaped and serves many varieties of pizza and pasta as well as English food, including Sunday roasts, chicken, veal, steaks and fish. There is a specials board and children are allowed in for food. It has been a pub for about 30 years and before that it was a club with a heliport at the rear! As a free house it offers a good range of ales such as Robinsons Best, HSB, Ruddles County, Royal Oak, Old Dray and local Tongham beers together with a selection of popular bottled beers and lagers and country wines. There is a large garden to the rear and a substantial car park where walkers may leave their cars with permission. Opening times are from 11.00-23.00 daily except Sunday when the usual hours of 12.00-15.00 and 19.00-22.30 apply. Food can be ordered between 12.00-22.00 on all days except Sundays when the ordering times are 12.00-14.00 and 19.00-21.30. Cold food is served on weekdays and Saturdays between 14.30-18.00.
Tel 0252 792050

The Mariners Hotel at Frensham

after his family name. Richard Combe, mentioned earlier, bought the house in 1864 and set up a breeding stud for thoroughbred horses. He died in 1900 although his widow stayed on, the house remaining with the Combe family until the last war.

Frensham Church, founded in 1239, is dedicated to St. Mary the Virgin and was formerly a chapelry of Farnham Church within the diocese of Winchester. The church occupies a hill top site and it certainly would have replaced an older church, although no trace has been found of this earlier building. A massively buttressed 14th Century tower stands at the western end of the church which is built of local sandstone and flint. Inside you will find an ancient square font dating from the 12th Century, possibly transferred from the earlier church. For centuries it lay outside in the churchyard, only being restored to its rightful position in 1875. The organ was given to the church in 1871 by Mrs Esther Combe of Pierrepont. Another item of interest is the massive cauldron of beaten copper standing on a tripod. It is 9ft in circumference, twelve inches deep, holds 100 gallons of water and is over 400 years old. It was probably part of the kitchen equipment of nearby Waverley Abbey.

Both Frensham ponds can be seen from this walk, the Great Pond being the largest sheet of water in

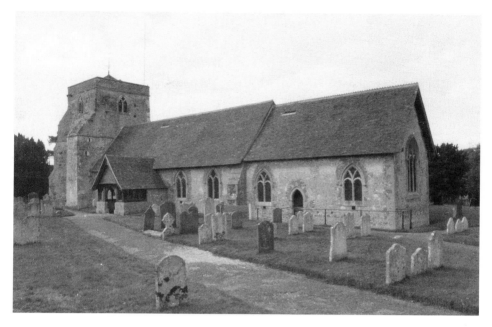

Frensham Church

Surrey. Created by the Bishops of Winchester they were stocked with pike, perch, roach, carp, tench and eels, the larger pond being excavated in 1208 or before and the smaller in 1246. Both ponds were drained during the Second World War so that they could not be used as a navigational aid by German pilots. The fish were relocated as draining took place. An early floatplane was tested on the Great Pond in 1913.

Walk 17

Distance: *Allow three hours for this walk of five miles*
From the parking area at the north side of the pub, look for a sign and a path which sidles alongside the building past a little bow window and heads westwards. Follow the path up to a stile at the top of a sharp rise with a glade on your left which must be a mass of bluebells in May. Cross the stile into a meadow and keeping the fence on your right, follow a well marked path until a hedge closes in obliquely on your left. Pass a stile on your right and proceed half left downhill over a meadow to some trees, ignoring all other paths. At the lower corner of the field, veer left over a metal railed footbridge and then climb a delightful sunken path up to a farm, where you follow a track for a few yards before joining a path on your left as the track veers right. This path shortly crosses a drive and soon plunges downhill through holly, bending right to meet a metalled track. Turn left here and

cross the southern branch of the River Wey by a footbridge. The river keeps you company for a little while until your path veers left and becomes a narrow lane. Swans, geese and a llama were cohabiting around a circular pond on our left as we passed.

The lane rises gently to The Street where you turn right alongside the church wall. The church is interesting and well worth a visit. On the other side of the road, stone cottages with brick quoins stand close to St Mary's Hall facing the church. Follow the road to Frensham Mill passing the black painted metal security gates of Frensham Manor. Do not cross the river but pass through the double gated entrance to the Georgian-style Old Mill House on your left and cross the frontal courtyard, leaving by way of a wooden gate directly ahead. This route is signed as a public bridleway to the right of the double gates as you enter from the road. Your path passes right of a well tended yew hedge with a house beyond. Dogs may bark at you as you pass alongside a garden wall and there is a sign warning horseriders of this hazard. Pass an arched footbridge before the river twists right, leaving you to follow a little stream draining Frensham Great Pond. A little way ahead the paths divides temporarily before joining again. The left hand fork is the bridleway which hugs the fence while the other dips to stream level beneath oaks and alders. If you use the latter, ignore the footbridge on your right and veer left to rejoin the bridleway.

Soon you reach Bacon Lane and Frensham Great Pond comes into view. Turn left and then shortly swing right away from the lane and on to a wide pond-side footpath. Enjoy your stroll alongside the pond which, centuries ago, used to be stocked with coarse fish for the Episcopal tables of Winchester but now is dotted at weekends with numerous dinghies. Soon fencing forces you inland to the car park but then turn right and resume your acquaintance with the pond. If you wish to visit the Information Centre or use the toilets, these lie to your left. The notice board here provides information on the latest bird sightings for the keen 'twitchers' in your party. Great Grey Shrike, Bittern and Cetti's Warbler amongst others had been seen near the pond when we passed.

Resuming the walk you will find directions hereabouts a little confusing, but if you head half left obliquely away from the pond, after you have turned right from the car park back to its sandy banks, and head towards some low metal railings (the boundary of a former car park), proceeding on the same alignment with railings on your right, you will meet a junction of four railed paths. Take the third path clockwise and head towards the main road and two isolated silver birch trees. The sand is deep here which makes walking difficult. Veer half left and cross the main road by the bus stops following a clearly defined path to the top of a ridge on Frensham Common. Pause here and look back to savour the view over Frensham Great Pond. Cross over a track and proceed through a barrier to meet another track. Veer a little to the left and pick up a narrower path on the right. Admire the views towards Frensham Little Pond and Crooksbury Hill as you descend through heather and gorse to a bridleway. Turn right here on a loose and

Walk 17

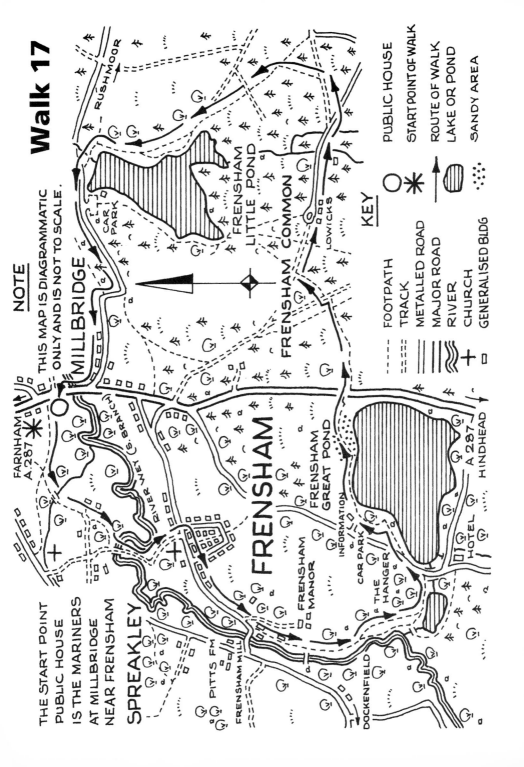

NOTE

THIS MAP IS DIAGRAMMATIC ONLY AND IS NOT TO SCALE.

THE START POINT PUBLIC HOUSE IS THE MARINERS AT MILLBRIDGE NEAR FRENSHAM

KEY

– – – –	FOOTPATH
⸗⸗⸗⸗	TRACK
‖‖‖‖	METALLED ROAD
‖‖	MAJOR ROAD
∿∿∿	RIVER
✝	CHURCH
▯	GENERALISED BLDG

○   PUBLIC HOUSE
✳   START POINT OF WALK
➤   ROUTE OF WALK
▭   LAKE OR POND
⋮   SANDY AREA

RUSHMOOR
MILLBRIDGE
FARNHAM A 287
CAR PARK
FRENSHAM LITTLE POND
FRENSHAM COMMON
LOWICKS
RIVER WEY (S. BRANCH)
SPREAKLEY
FRENSHAM
FRENSHAM MANOR
FRENSHAM GREAT POND
INFORMATION
CAR PARK
THE HANGER
A 287 HINDHEAD
HOTEL
DOCKENFIELD
FRENSHAM MILL
PITTS FM

sandy track which soon becomes a little firmer and then metalled as you reach Smugglers Cottage (an ideal isolated cottage for the storing of contraband!). Follow the lane past other dwellings through a ford (if you don't have your wellies, use the adjacent footbridge!). Shortly cross another stream soon forking left along a track indicated by a public bridleway sign.

Continue slightly uphill through young pines until you see a distinct path forking left through the trees. Follow this and shortly join another path through a gap in the wire fence. Turn left and soon pass through the fields of a coniferous tree nursery along a fenced path eventually passing a National Trust sign for Frensham Little Pond. After this take a left-hand path under birch, pine and oak keeping the pond to your left. Shortly you will meet the main path again as the trees begin to thin out and fine views of the pond open up on your left. At

Dusk over Frensham Great Pond

the pond's end veer left under a fine looking oak to follow the pond's northern edge behind a retaining wall, briefly dipping down to cross the pond's outfall. With a reedy area to your left take a path turning left under an oak tree whose spreading roots are very exposed and soon join a metalled lane. Follow the lane left-handed under pine and birch past two car parks and round a double bend (take good care here) looking out for the attractive cottages on the right before emerging on to the A287 by the old Post Office. Turn right, cross the Wey and back to The Mariners.

Heights and fine views from Thursley

WALK 18
Allow 4 hours
6 miles
Walk begins page 110

Background to the Walk

Tucked away in a valley with the wooded crest of Hindhead away to the south, lies the unspoilt village of Thursley. Apart from a little modern development south of the church, not much has changed over the years. The faint buzz of traffic on A3 to the east does not affect the quiet charm of the village.

Thursley is derived from 'Thunor's Leah' which is Anglo-Saxon for ' a clearing of thunor or Thor' — a heathen god. At the village centre lies the well-maintained triangular green which contains two acacia trees planted in 1934 in memory of that farmer, politician, writer and traveller on horseback William Cobbett. He was born a few miles away at Farnham and died not far away at Normandy Farm to the north of the Hogs Back. He liked Thursley, staying in the village on occasions. Acacia trees had a particular fascination for him and explains the choice of this memorial. A sign on the green explains the derivation of the village name and serves as a memorial to Bill Cooper, one-time parish councillor and clerk.

Outside the well kept village hall is a tall metal sign which announces that Thursley is Surrey's best kept village. These awards are normally made annually but the sign is undated. However, dates abound at the church of St Michael and all Angels set upon its hillside, the oldest part being Saxon with Norman extensions and the inevitable Victorian alterations. Look for the sundial on the bell tower bearing the inscription 'Hora pars vitae' meaning ' an hour is a part of life'. Massive timber framing supports the tower from the nave of the church and is said to be the finest example

Maps
Landranger 1:50,000
Sheet 186
Pathfinder 1:25,000
Sheet 1245 SU83/93
Map Reference of Start/
Finish SU903397

How to get there
From Farnham take B3001 southwards over the signalled junction with A31 and continue for nearly 4 miles to Elstead where you turn right at the triangular green, proceeding past the church for a further two miles before turning left for Thursley. Continue into the village to the Three Horseshoes which lies to the right up an access road a little way beyond the triangular village green. From Camberley follow A325 until you meet A31 at the large roundabout east of Farnham. Turn right and follow A31 westwards to the traffic lights where you turn left to follow B3001. Continue as above to Thursley. The restricted Stagecoach service 274 runs from Hindhead to Guildford via Thursley. Stagecoach services 219 and 519 will connect with service 274 at Hindhead but it would be wise to check with the Company's office on 0428 605727 first. Alternatively the walk could be joined at Gibbett Hill,

Hindhead by using the services from Farnham. From Camberley proceed on Tillingbourne through service F40 to Farnham and join the Hindhead services there.

Pub facilities
Three Horseshoes, Thursley

The former Red Lion pub in Thursley where travellers refreshed themselves for the long ascent to Hindhead is no more, but The Three Horseshoes fills the void quite handsomely. It has been a pub since 1927 and the former old cottage at the rear of the building is 300 years old. The newer front facade has a tile hung upper storey while the ground floor is attractively built of local stone laid in herring bone fashion with brick quoins. Tall chimneys match the architecture. The pub is a free house and its special ales include Gales' BBB and HSB. There is also Scrumpy Jack, Beamish Irish Stout, Carling and Tennents lagers together with bottled beers and a selection of Gales country wines. The bar is quite small and cosy with a patterned carpet and a beamed red ceiling. There are fireplaces at either end, each mounted with three horseshoes and three polo sticks adorn one of the walls. The landlord values his local customers and to protect their interests he has a notice on the door saying We regret that walkers in groups of five or more strictly by appointment only. A blackboard lists bar food with home cooked pies, leek bacon and mushroom gratin and salmon pasta bake tempting us when we called. Folding doors

The Three Horseshoes at Thursley

in Surrey, while the font is a good example of Saxon work. Nearby, the parish chest dates from 1622.

In the churchyard is a sailor's grave and his tragic story is recounted upon the gravestone. He was murdered by three men he befriended at the former Red Lion pub at Thursley, the foul deed being committed at Hindhead on the Portsmouth Road in September 1786. The three men were apprehended at the Flying Bull at Liss in Hampshire after a gun fight and were hung in chains on Gibbett Hill which you visit on this walk. Near the unfortunate seafarer's grave lies the poet John Freeman, the field just over the church wall being given to the National Trust in his memory.

During this walk you pass over the wooded heights of Hindhead, once a wild and dangerous area, much dreaded by travellers on the Old Portsmouth Road. Samuel Pepys, travelling in 1668, engaged a guide to conduct him between Guildford and Petersfield. However, Professor John Tyndall, an eminent scientist in the 19th Century, can be said to be the founder of modern Hindhead. He thought the air here was superb and built his house there with others taking the hint, including George Bernard Shaw and Sir Arthur Conan Doyle, the latter lived in what is now the Undershaw Hotel. Shops and villas sprung up and The Royal Huts Hotel was one of the earliest buildings. Sadly this is no more, but the locals still refer to the area around the crossroads as The Huts. What a great relief it was in

The village green and Cobbett's Acacia trees

1993 when the Department of Transport announced a tunnel under Hindhead for the A3 improvements.

You will have a fine view of that famous deep hollow, circumvented by the A3, called The Devil's Punchbowl. An earlier name was the less spectacular Haccombe (or Highcombe) Bottom. On the return part of the walk you will tread the route of the Old Portsmouth Road and see how the track has been hollowed out by innumerable cart wheels, horses' hooves and human feet over the years.

Finally, I should tell you that the ascent to Gibbett Hill is steep and unrelenting and you may be disconcerted to find many people strolling around on the summit looking quite relaxed. You can say that you did it the hard way while they used a car and the nearby car park, but you will have gained greater satisfaction and be able to appreciate the view from the top much more as a result.

lead to a restaurant where the evening menu changes regularly. Food can be ordered from 12.00-14.00 and 19.00-21.00 daily. Opening times are 11.00-14.30 (Mon-Thurs), 1100-15.00 (Fri-Sat) and 12.00-15.00 (Sun). Evening times are 18.00-23.00 and 19.00-22.30 Sundays. Children are not allowed in the bar but may use the restaurant or the very large garden. There is a car park outside the pub but on busy days you may have to go 300 yards down the raod and park by the cricket ground.
Tel 0252 703268.

Walk 18

Distance: *Allow four hours for this walk of six miles*

Note: There is a steep climb up Gibbett Hill on this walk. From the Three Horseshoes turn left and head down to the road looking out for the gabled village hall to your right. Go forward to the green taking the road to your left noting Cobbett's two acacia trees and Bill Cooper's memorial on the green to your right. Follow the lane down past farm buildings and look out for the delightful Sunset Cottage on your left and more charming cottages further along. As the lane goes right up towards the church (you can have a look at the church either now or when you return) take a sunken bridleway to your left by a four-armed footpath sign. Follow this to where it turns right to Rack Close and look for a weighted gate to your left by a stile and a wooden bridleway sign (ignore an earlier metal footpath sign on your left). Take the alignment indicated by the bridleway sign diagonally right across the meadow towards the left-hand edge of a hedge. As you go along you should detect a faint path which guides you to another weighted gate. Proceed along a fenced path to meet and cross the dual carriageway A3.

Continue along a lane banked on each side, passing the gate to Cosford House, which eventually comes into view prettily on your left shortly before the lane descends into a valley. As the lane turns left, take a track to the right by a three armed bridleway sign and follow this track up the valley passing Hole Cottage (which may now be open for coffee, lunches or teas) to a junction of tracks. Turn left and proceed uphill under holly and oaks ignoring a right turning track. Soon you descend and pass a pond where a few mallards paddled lazily around as we passed. Signs warn of the dangers of swimming here because of deep mud but we were not tempted, as a chill north westerly breeze blew up the valley.

The track climbs through holly, birch and beech over a crest passing another track and a footpath sign to the right. Continue ahead along a fenced track passing the attractive Halnacker buildings to your left before you go gently downhill to meet a metalled lane. As you do so, a pleasant oak clad knoll appears on the left with a footpath running up towards it. Follow the lane right-handed and at the far twist of an S bend take a look at the beautiful Halnacker Cottage with its lych-type gate, distinctive porch, lovely garden and pond. What lucky people live in idyllic places like this!

Tear yourself away and proceed uphill to a road junction where you go left, over the brow of a hill and down to another road junction. Take the minor road on the left and continue for about 200 yards to where a footpath sign points right handed into the trees. There is also a Polana house sign at the beginning of this path. Initially this path becomes muddy but drier conditions prevail as you reach a path junction just after passing some farm buildings. Cross the junction and proceed directly ahead on a gravel track between two gate pillars with Roundles Cottage on the left. Pass a vehicle turning area and continue uphill on a path which initially veers slightly to the right through trees with a little gully on your right.

You have now begun the tree shrouded climb to the summit of Gibbett Hill, 272

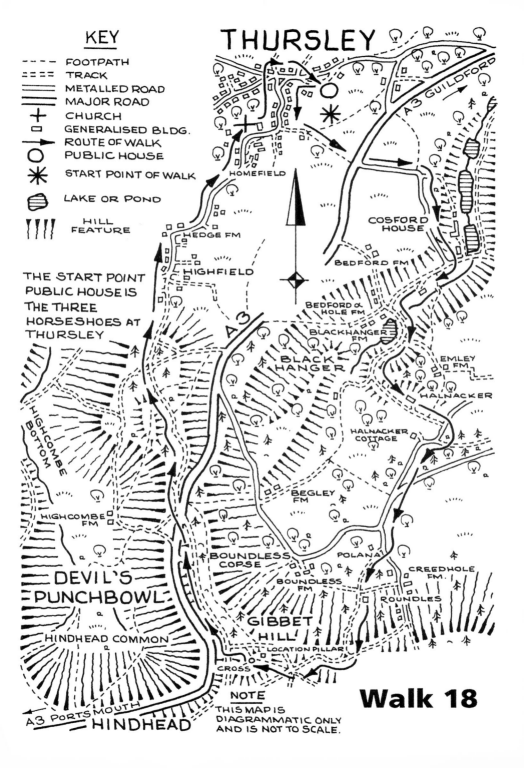

metres or 892 feet above sea level. We paused frequently on this climb which is severe in places. The path makes its way up to a junction where there is a marker post. Turn right here and toil uphill eventually reaching the junction of six tracks, a marker post on your left has all six paths marked by arrows. Your path is the one with a wooden horse barrier half right from where you stand.

Thursley Church

Continue the uphill slog and shortly take the left hand fork where the path divides. Where the path divides again by a marker post take the right hand fork and presently emerge on to the summit of grass and heather. Absorb the stunning view to Guildford, The Hogs back and Leith Hill to the north. A rest on one of the seats may be welcome before carrying on. Look at the concrete location pillar and then walk over to the Celtic style cross inscribed in Latin and erected by Lord Chief Justice Earle in 1851.

From this point, with your back to the concrete location pillar mentioned above, ignore the well trodden track leading straight ahead and take a lesser path leading half right down through heather into stunted birch and oak (There is a marker post with a yellow arrow in full view on the right hand side of the path). At the bottom, pass through the wooden horse barrier turning left and then right at a T junction of tracks. Follow this gently downhill with the noise of A3 traffic below on the left backed by the canyon-like Devil's Punch Bowl. Ignore all side turnings and eventually cross with care the single carriageway A3 and then follow the continuation track ahead ignoring the initial left turning track.

Follow the track gently downhill and you will note that, as you finally leave the heather, bracken, birch and pines behind, your track becomes very sunken even continuing in this fashion when you reach the metalled lane by the Highfield farms. This was the old Portsmouth Road used by many travellers in times gone by. From the Highfield farms follow the pleasant winding lane past Hedge Farm with its mellow local sandstone and brick quoins until the houses of Thursley appear. Shortly after passing the 30 mph sign there is a massive oak on your left and after this look for Strensall on the right where there is a path you can follow for a while to avoid walking on the road. Go past the church and back to the village green turning right and back to the Three Horseshoes.

Woodland paths & a deserted village from Oakhanger

WALK 19
Allow 3 ½ hours
5 ½ miles
Walk begins page 115

Background to the Walk

To the west, the wooded slopes of the hangers brood distantly over the houses of Oakhanger, while to the east, the stream bearing the name of the village glides through its meadowland, acting as a barrier between rural Oakhanger and military Bordon. In hanger country it is feasible to assume that Oakhanger means just what it says — 'An oakwood upon a hillside', but it may have different origins. An earlier spelling of 'ochangre' suggest that it may have been a spring or a pond near a hanger. The present village spreads itself thinly along the road from Kingsley to Blackmoor and is probably not much different in character to when Gilbert White of nearby Selborne called it 'a string of farms and scattered houses along the verge of the forest'. This was in the days when Alice Holt and Woolmer Forest were much more extensive than they are today.

Times, however, have changed at Oakhanger with the Ministry of Defence playing a prominent part. A site bordering the village to the west was developed as a wireless station at the start of the Second World War. So good was the art of camouflage that the site resembled a ploughed field from the air. Now it resembles a miniature Fylingdales with green and white 'golf balls' intruding upon the pastoral landscape, and a third over towards Bordon. Similar to, but smaller than those at Goonhilly in Cornwall, the 'golf balls' contain satellite and radar dishes to transmit and receive messages from satellites in space for the Royal Aerospace Establishment Telemetry and Command Station. To protect equipment from the weather, the housing is

Maps
Landranger 1:50,000
Sheet 186
Pathfinder 1:25,000
Sheet 1224 SU63/73
Map Reference of Start/
Finish SU769359

How to get there
Take West Street out of Farnham crossing A31 at the roundabout to follow A325 through Wrecclesham and Alice Holt Forest to where B3004 goes right towards Alton. Follow th is through Kingsley and take the Oakhanger Road which turns left off B3004. You will find the Red Lion on your right after a mile. From Camberley follow A325 to the large roundabout east of Farnham where you turn right and follow A31 westbound to the roundabout junction with A325 west of Farnham. Follow A325 left-handed and proceed as above. Oakhanger is served by Stagecoach and Hampshire Bus restricted service no 212 which plys between Liphook and Alton. From Farnham take regular services 518 (Stagecoach and Guildford/West Surrey), 226 (Oakley Coaches) or 18 (Stagecoach) alighting at Bordon Camp Fire Station and joining service 212 there. Check with Stagecoach on

0252 23322 *first. From Camberley take any of the many regular services to Aldershot Bus Station (Stagecoach 20, 20A 24 or 24A) and pick up the above mentioned services 18, 226 or 518 via Farnham to Bordon where you join service 212 as above.*

Pub facilities
Red Lion,
Oakhanger

Agreeably placed behind a small forecourt at a junction of lanes, the Red Lion offers a pleasingly uneven face to the visitor. The interest is maintained inside with a small, cosy lounge bar and an even cosier restaurant area. The spacious public bar to the right offers television and more modern entertainment. Sit in the lounge bar alongside the inglenook fireplace with its genuine log fire, surrounded by copper and brass ornaments and enjoy the range of Courage ales supported by John Smiths bitter. There are also alternate guest ales of Old Dray (brewed at nearby East Worldham) and Ringwood 49. Kronenberg and Fosters lagers are also on offer, all to be enjoyed during the opening times of 11.00-15.00 and 18.00-23.00 (Mon-Sat) and 12.00-15.00, 19.00-22.30 (Sun). If you fancy food, enjoy that too from the extensive menu. The pub specialises in fresh fish, so choose from 9 varieties ranging from brill to lemon sole. The snack menu is varied (from brunch to hickory chicken) with 6 types of omelette, 4 basket meals and a huge range of sandwiches, not forgetting burgers and ploughmans. The restaurant

The Red Lion at Oakhanger

made from a plastic membrane supported on a lattice framework.

Down to earth now and about a quarter of a mile along the Kingsley road from the Red Lion pub is the brick built village church facing the green. £600 was the cost of building it in 1868 but only occasional services are held there now. There was a time when the nave was actually used as a school and only the chancel was dedicated. Opposite to the church lies Shortheath Common containing a large pond amid trees and scrubland. Wild life abounds around and in the pond — a 32lb pike was once pulled from the depths and the fish is now on display at the Red Lion.

There is a very different story to another village you will encounter on the walk. When you reach the site of the former village of Hartley Mauditt, look around and you will see vague mounds in the meadow, a pond, and a church standing defiantly alone. The manor was held by William Mauditt at the time of Domesday and valued at £7. The manor house used to stand in the trees to the west of the church and a group of about ten cottages formed part of the estate. It was classed as a village in 1316 and eventually became the property of the Earl of Lancaster, passing to his son Henry who was created Duke of Lancaster in 1351. The end of Hartley Mauditt began in 1789 when the owner, the last Lord Stawell, decided to demolish the manor house against

Tunford Cottage at Oakhanger

menu is mouth watering but do ring up and book at weekends. Satisfy your palate between 11.00-14.30 and 18.00-22.30 (Mon-Sat), 12.00-15.00 and 19.00-22.00 (Sun). Formerly two cottages, the Red Lion has been a pub since 1760 and claims a 'brushing past' ghost in the kitchen. Although the building is listed, Alan Norris the cheerful host, has hopes of some extensions being approved. There is parking for 20 cars front and rear, but obtain permission to leave your car while you walk. Children are allowed in the two rear gardens and in the restaurant, but in the latter, they must be 8 years old and well-behaved. Tel 0420 472232.

the wishes of his wife, because he wished to live in London (and she wanted to stay in the country). With the demise of the house, there was little employment left in the village and sadly the cottages fell empty and were eventually demolished. A 'white lady' ghost is said to haunt the trees where the old manor house once stood — Lady Stawell still yearning for her country retreat?

The church of St. Leonards still stands and is a good example of Norman architecture, built in the 12th century with later additions by the Duke of Lancaster. The 15th Century font has Lancastrian roses carved into its sides, but the church bell cast in 1601 was stolen from its belfry over 20 years ago and has never been recovered. The church contains many monuments to the Stuart family who owned the manor in the 17th and 18th centuries.

On your outward route, you will pass the 18th Century Priory Farm standing on the site of the 13th Century Selborne Priory and built from the stones of the Priory. It was founded, in 1233 by Peter de Roche, Bishop of Winchester, for the Black Canons order of St Augustine. The Priory was dissolved in 1484 and fell into decay rapidly afterwards.

Walk 19

Distance: *Allow three-and-a-half hours for this walk of five-and-a-half miles*
As you leave the Red Lion, turn right and follow the road past the RAF station until you reach two fine timber and brick cottages, the second one called Tunford on the right. Cross the stile just past Tunford, keeping on the right hand side of an arable field into the corner and round to another stile. Cross this and turn left to follow the hedge line as near as possible. Leave this meadow by a stile near the field corner

and cross into the next meadow, maintaining your direction to cross the Oakhanger Stream on the far side and pass through a gap to enter the next meadow. Here you will find a five-armed footpath sign indicating a good choice of direction, but your route lies right to parallel the Oakhanger Stream. With a barbed wire fence to your right, cross over two stiles, the second of which is followed by a plank over a ditch.

Maintain your direction to cross another stile in the far hedge, again with a following plank. An arrow guides you over a further meadow to locate another stile in the opposite hedge, this one being preceded by a planked ditch. Now head slightly right to the corner of a wire fence, with woodland closing up on the right encasing the Oakhanger Stream. Maintain the wire fence on your left until your path takes on the mantle of an inferior farm track. As you pass through a gap in a wire fence ahead, look half right and locate a wooden footbridge, which you use to cross the stream. Keep the stream on your left and follow its course to a metal gate with Priory Farm across the stream to your left. Pass through the gate and turn right to follow a track towards Coombe Wood entering its shady recesses under canopies of oak and beech with a scattering of hazel and field maple. When you reach a track fork, branch left and cross a stile by a metal gate. Enter a field with scattered oaks and ash to your right heading slightly right to join a faint track on the field's far side. This veers right uphill with a bank on the left.

Two gates now confront you but choose the right-hand one signed Bridleway, following a sunken path uphill to pass Wick Hill Farm on the left. Continue on a metalled lane up to where it bends sharply right and is joined by a track from the left. Facing you is a gap in the hedge with a footpath sign on the right. Pass through the gap and proceed half left over arable land towards an electricity pole. When we walked the route there was a distinct path leading straight through knee high cereal crops. When you reach the pole, there is a two-armed footpath sign and a plank over a ditch. Maintain your direction over arable ground until you arrive at a waymarked post where you veer left and then shortly right parallel with a ditch, following this to a three armed footpath sign, where you go left and cross the ditch by way of a plank. Turn right and follow the hedgerow down to a lane via a gap in the hedge.

You now enter the area of the abandoned village of Hartley Mauditt where people once lived and worked for the lord of the manor. The church of St Nicholas stands as a last bastion, well-maintained but services are held in Summer only. The village pond is on your right, its banks ablaze with yellow iris and its surface dotted with water lilies when we passed. Follow the lane onwards up a slight incline passing Hartley Mauditt House on the right until you come to the buildings of West Worldham, looking out for a lane leading off right as you reach the attractive Cornerstone Cottage, also on your right. Follow this narrow, interesting lane and as it descends steeply off the hanger into a sharp left hand bend, turn right by a three armed footpath sign, taking the path alongside a wire fence with a meadow and distant woodland to the left. Cattle browsed lazily in the meadow during the warm June afternoon as we followed this path through fine hanger

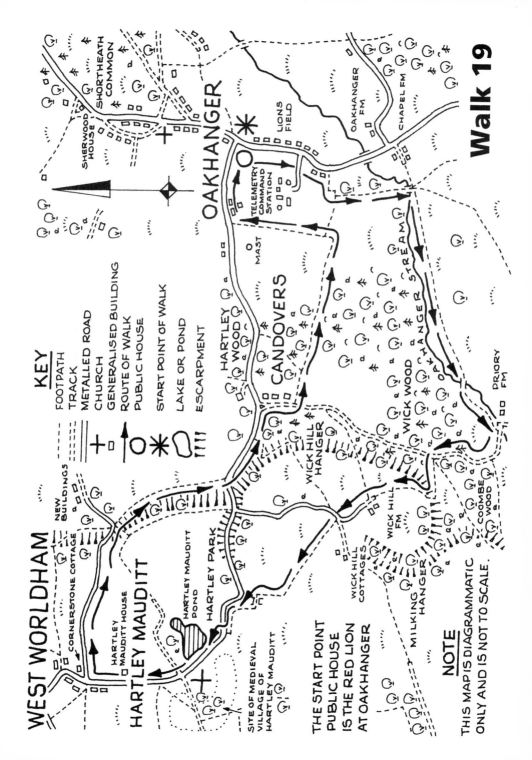

Walk 19

KEY

FOOTPATH
TRACK
METALLED ROAD
CHURCH
GENERALISED BUILDING
ROUTE OF WALK
PUBLIC HOUSE
START POINT OF WALK
LAKE OR POND
ESCARPMENT

NEW BUILDINGS

SHORTHEATH COMMON

SHERWOOD HOUSE

OAKHANGER

LIONS FIELD

TELEMETRY COMMAND STATION

MAST

OAKHANGER FM

CHAPEL FM

WEST WORLDHAM

CORNERSTONE COTTAGE

HARTLEY MAUDITT HOUSE

HARTLEY MAUDITT

HARTLEY MAUDITT POND

HARTLEY PARK

SITE OF MEDIEVAL VILLAGE OF HARTLEY MAUDITT

HARTLEY WOOD

CANDOVERS

WICK HILL HANGER

WICK WOOD

OAKHANGER STREAM

PRIORY FM

WICK HILL FM

WICK HILL COTTAGES

MILKING HANGER

COOMBE WOOD

THE START POINT PUBLIC HOUSE IS THE RED LION AT OAKHANGER

NOTE

THIS MAP IS DIAGRAMMATIC ONLY AND IS NOT TO SCALE.

country up to a lane, where we turned left in a downhill direction. Before long a lane appears on the right signposted Candovers. This is also the route of the 17-mile long scenic footpath between Alton and Petersfield called The Hangers Way. The Candovers are a small group of cottages which originally formed a part of the Hartley Mauditt estate. The 1881 census listed five cottages here, one of which was once called home by the estate carpenter.

Turning right into the lane, you pass High Candover and Long Candovers before the lane becomes a gravelled track. Immediately after a large converted thatched wooden barn (the mind boggles at possible insurance premiums!), a footpath sign points your way left-handed over a stile and alongside a wire fence until you enter Hartley Wood by means of a wooden pedestrian gate. Follow the well-defined path down through

St Nicholas Church, Hartley Mauditt

mixed woodland, after first ignoring a lesser used path branching left just after the gate. As the lower boundary of the wood comes into sight, veer right on to a green avenue and immediately left to surmount two stepless stiles. With the green and white 'golf balls' of the Royal Aerospace Establishment in view, take the path down the right-hand side of a large arable field and follow the hedge round to the left in the corner, ignoring a stile on your right. Proceed along the lower edge of the field with initially a hedge, then a barbed-wire fence and finally a ditch on your right. It was here that we disturbed a roe deer which leapt out of its hiding place in the ditch and shot away in graceful bounds to woodland cover. What beautiful, lithe creatures they are! Cross over a stile, followed by a plank footbridge and leave the field by another stile followed by another footbridge to reach a lane. Follow this right-handed past Hartleywood Farm back to the Red Lion.

Valley lakes and heathland from Hammer Vale

WALK 20
Allow 3 hours
5 miles
Walk begins page 121

Background to the Walk

As the high western Weald comes to a climax in the deeply-furrowed hills centred on Hindhead, we find ourselves in the valley of the infant southern branch of the River Wey. The infant begins its journey to the Thames by flowing south west and then twisting around the western bastions of Hindhead to end up flowing north east to join the river's northern branch at Tilford. In this valley we find the village of Hammer, just inside the County of West Sussex but within a stone's throw of Surrey and Hampshire. Trains roar up and down the Hammer valley, the line being opened between London and Portsmouth in 1848 after several years of construction. The line was called the Portsmouth Direct to differentiate it from other railway lines between London and Portsmouth which took other, more devious routes. The line passes through some very difficult terrain which resulted in construction problems with many bends and gradients. Electrification of the line in the form of a third rail came to the Portsmouth Direct in 1936. Trains coming up the valley to Haslemere negotiate a gradient of 1:100 but there are steeper sections of 1:80 in other parts.

The name Hammer is significant, as before the Industrial Revolution, this Wealden countryside was once the heartland of the iron industry. Although it is quiet and residential now, it was not always so. Once, these valleys were full of the acrid smell of charcoal fired forges and the clang of blacksmiths' hammers echoed up the valley sides in a landscape littered with ash. The crash of the blacksmith's hammer is how the village got its name and there were plenty of them at

Maps
Landranger 1:50,000
Sheet 186
Pathfinder 1:25,000
Sheet 1245 SU83/93
Map Reference of Start/
Finish SU868326

How to get there
From Farnham take A287 to Hindhead where you turn right on to A3 southbound at the traffic lights. Follow A3 straight ahead until you reach the dual carriageway. At this point tak e the side road to the left (Sandy Lane) and at the cross roads keep straight ahead on Sandy Lane down the valley to a road junction. Turn right here on to Hammer Lane and the Prince of Wales is on your right after a quarter mile. From Camberley take A325 to the large roundabout east of Farnham where you turn right and follow A31 westbound to the traffic lights. Follow the signing left here for A287 Hindhead and then proceed as above. There is no bus service in Hammer Lane past the Prince of Wales but local Stagecoach regular service 502 running between Grayswood and Linchmere via Haslemere Station and Hammer Vale passes the top end of Hammer Lane where you alight and walk the quarter mile to the pub. From

Farnham services 219 and 519 (Stagecoach/Guildford and West Surrey) run to Haslemere Station where you can join service 502. From Camberley, many services (including Stagecoach 20, 20A, 24 and 24A) run to Aldershot Bus Station where you can join services 219 or 519 and proceed as above.

Pub facilities
Prince of Wales,
Hammer Vale
Built in 1927, the pub looks a little incongruous in this valley with a narrow, twisting lane linking scattered houses. Its substantial appearance does not harmonise at all well in its surroundings but there is a reason for this. When it was built, there were plans for the A3 trunk road to be re-routed up this valley on its way to Guildford from Petersfield. That fortunately was not to be, so the wide brick pub front looks down the valley with some embarrassment. The pub was scheduled for redecoration shortly after we visited but the hammered glass windows with coloured glass lettering are thankfully not scheduled for change. These glass insets announce the 'Smoking Room', 'Public Bar' and 'Luncheons and Teas' in the fashion of early 20th Century town pubs. It is a Gales house offering HSB, BBB and Gales Best with stouts, lagers and ciders available, together with a range of Gales home made wines. The pub is open from 11.00-15.00 and 18.00-23.00 (Mon-Sat) with normal Sunday opening hours. There ia a good range of food with two menus (one main and one snack) and a pizza menu

The Prince of Wales at Hammer Vale

the iron mill in Pophole which worked for nearly 200 years from the 16th to the 18th Centuries. Nearby Shottermill is named after the Shotter family and their iron industry. The family mansion can be found on the Fernhurst Road built for the iron master William Shotter, with the date 1687 over the main door.

Local ironstone was dug out of pits and smelted in furnaces and forges using charcoal as a fuel. A circular pit or hearth was dug and a pole erected centrally. Locally chopped wood was stacked up against the pole and then clay was packed tightly around the wood until it was covered. A fire was started and the extraction of iron from iron ore was achieved by a smouldering fire watched over night and day to ensure that it did not burst into flames. A typical forge could take a week to burn out. Iron ore smelting in this fashion was not new in the area as the Romans used similar methods well over a thousand years earlier. Later forges used water as the motive power for the hammers, which resulted in a scattering of hammer ponds in the district. The most famous and now the most picturesque of these, are the three ponds of Waggoners (or Wakeners) Wells which you pass on the walk. Henry Hooke formed these by damming Cooper's stream and he was in the favoured position of possessing endless supplies of iron ore, timber galore for charcoal and as much water as he wanted. He started his business in the early 17th

Gillham's Farm — fine example of an English farmhouse

which is not available on Sundays. The pub tends to specialise in Mexican dishes with tortillas and spicy chicken in evidence. Other dishes are a little more commonplace with grills, chicken dishes, omelettes, burgers and vegetarian meals to choose from. A blackboard displays the desserts which included creme caramel. Satisfy your appetite between 12.00-13.50 and 19.00-21.50 each day. There is a large car park and a terraced garden beyond which merges with the heathland on the valley side. Walkers may leave their cars with permission. Children are welcome in the left-hand bar which is loosely termed a restaurant.

Tel 0428 652600

Century and as he conveniently owned all the surrounding land he overcame the problem presented by the Act of 1585 under which the owner of any new iron works was requires to provide timber for charcoal from his own land.

Iron ore smelting and the forge industry were not the only activities carried out in the vicinity of Hammer. There were also tile and brick works, which utilised local clays of separate blue and yellow hues to produce tiles and bricks respectively. Many local houses have been bricked and tiled by using the products of the Hammer brickworks. The business faded in 1938 when clay supplies finally ran out after nearly 200 years.

Not satisfied with iron, brick and tile industries, Hammer and the Upper Wey valleys indulged in broom making by utilising the vast amount of birch trees in the deep valleys. The brooms were of a very high quality and were traditionally used in the Royal stables. This area was England's Black Country before Wolverhampton, Walsall and West Bromwich claimed the name, but is now a haven of peaceful valleys and tree-clad slopes. Beautiful buildings abound, one of which, Gillhams Farm, you pass on the walk. Although not a building of great historical significance, it is an attractive and well-preserved example of a late-16th Century English farmhouse.

Walk 20

Distance: *Allow three hours for this walk of five miles*

Leave the pub and turn left into Hammer Lane, then almost immediately hard right by a footpath sign. Follow a track past Riverside Cottage and then cross both the River Wey and the railway, through a farmyard and on to a metalled road. Where this turns left, you turn right over a stile keeping the hedge on your right until you enter woodland by way of a small gate. There is a bungalow to your left and a Private sign to your right which you ignore, as this is a public right of way. This is Gillhams Moor Wood and is administered by the Woodland Trust. Where the path forks by a sign, keep left and climb through deciduous woodland, to pass through a wooden gate and with a grassy bank to the right, pass through another gate to join a path where your route is right-handed.

Spare a couple of moments however, to cross the lane to your left and admire Gillhams Farm, a model of charm in immaculate surroundings as we looked. Retrace your steps and proceed down a fenced path with East Lodge on your left. After a footpath joins yours from the right you soon turn right to pass under the railway by a brick arched bridge as a track joins from the left. A board walk and a bridge takes you over the River Wey before you toil uphill to join Hammer Lane at the entrance to Hewshott House on the left. Parts of the house are 16th Century but this has been covered by a later structure dated about 1910. Turn left uphill on Hammer Lane and after a left hand bend, look for an access road leading right signed to Old Barn Farm. Follow this road, turning right with it as it passes Old Barn and then Old Barn Farm which is now a Caravan Club House. Look out for a garage type building on your left and turn left immediately you have passed it. Do not enter the caravan field which lies straight ahead. Follow this track, which becomes a path, down and then up to meet a cross path with a three-armed foot path sign where you turn right to follow a pleasant, winding common edge path, ignoring all side paths until you reach the entrance to Upper Fold. Turn left here and head away from the gate on a gravel track which shortly joins another from the right. Proceed through thinned out woodland until you meet a metalled access road, where you continue directly ahead towards the roar of traffic on A3. Follow the road as it turns left up to a wooden gate. Do not pass through the wooden gate but turn right and cross the A3 dual carriageway with care, to join a side road leading away opposite.

Silver birch shades this road as it descends and rises again before another road joins from the left. Proceed straight ahead to where the metalling ends at a small car park with a bungalow called Parklands on your left. Follow the path on the left of the car park to a dry valley. Various paths lead up the bank on the far side of the valley, but take the sunken path on the extreme left which is soft going in places. As you reach a path divergence, take the left fork and move downhill to cross a footbridge to your left over Coopers Stream. On the far side, turn right and you will shortly discover a wishing well on the left where you can toss a coin into the shallow well. This will be retrieved in due course by the National Trust and used for the maintenance of Ludshott Common which includes Waggoners Wells.

Continue on the path and soon the lower pond of the three that comprise Waggoners Wells appears. Look to the left to see the quarry where rock and soil was excavated to form the dam. This feature is repeated at the lower end of each of the two other ponds. Follow the path past the larger middle pond to the far end of the upper and smaller pond, where you meet a road and turn right over a ford.

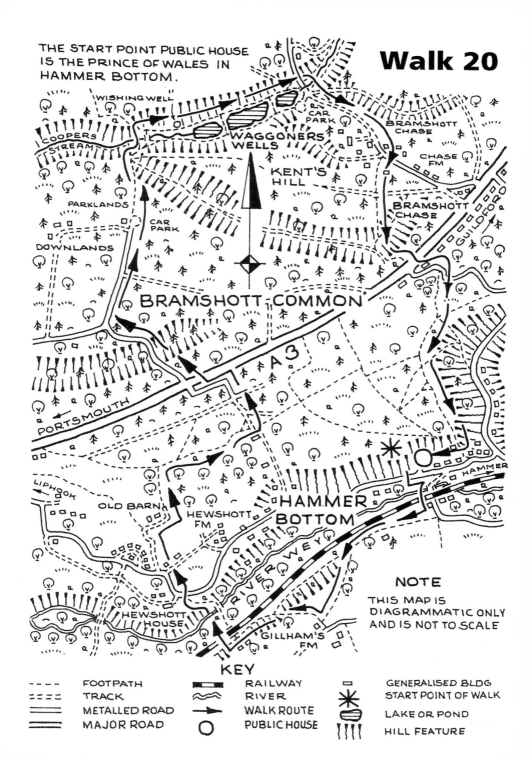

THE START POINT PUBLIC HOUSE IS THE PRINCE OF WALES IN HAMMER BOTTOM.

Walk 20

WISHING WELL

COOPERS STREAM

CAR PARK

WAGGONERS WELLS

BRAMSHOTT CHASE

CHASE FM

KENT'S HILL

BRAMSHOTT CHASE

PARKLANDS

CAR PARK

DOWNLANDS

GUILDFO

BRAMSHOTT COMMON

A3

PORTSMOUTH

HAMMER

LIPHOOK

OLD BARN

HEWSHOTT FM

HAMMER BOTTOM

RIVER WEY

NOTE

THIS MAP IS DIAGRAMMATIC ONLY AND IS NOT TO SCALE

HEWSHOTT HOUSE

GILLHAM'S FM

KEY

- - - -	FOOTPATH	▬▬	RAILWAY	▭	GENERALISED BLDG
=====	TRACK	∼∼	RIVER	✳	START POINT OF WALK
≡≡≡	METALLED ROAD	→	WALK ROUTE		
≡≡≡	MAJOR ROAD	○	PUBLIC HOUSE	⬭	LAKE OR POND
				ⵊⵊⵊ	HILL FEATURE

As the road turns right up to a car park, bear left on a signed bridleway and immediately take the right hand fork where the track divides.

A hard slog uphill now follows under beech, holly and oak before you pass Bramshot Chase House to the right, as the going becomes easier and your track becomes metalled at Clock House. A little further along, look for a pea gravel drive turning right opposite to a footpath sign and by a house sign for Three Firs. Carry on to where the drive forks by a three-armed footpath sign and take the path to the left of a hedge topped wall alongside a lawn. Your route becomes clear as the path becomes hedge-bordered and leads through a gate out on to a common. The path is well-defined through bracken, gorse and scattered silver birch. Soon you cross a track and another path before descending to the valley floor where you meet another path and turn right. Make your way through trees to meet a track which

Sad-looking donkey at Hammer Bottom

you follow left and go uphill through silver birch. Where the track fades, swing left as you hear A3 traffic through gorse bushes ahead to reach the verge of the main road by crossing a ditch on the right.

Cross the dual carriageway, again with care and enter a lane just above the old Venue Restaurant — closed and shuttered as we passed. Follow the lane past the Little Chef around a right-hand bend where you follow a signed path into bushes on the right. With a wood to your right, you arrive at a three-armed footpath sign and turn right to follow a wide grassy path beneath power lines. Ignore all side paths until a slight veer to the right opens up a wide green swathe into the distance with power lines above. At this point, look for a left turning path through silver birch, indicated by a marker post. Follow this across another path and fork left as the path divides, descending through gorse to a path crossing with a two-armed footpath sign. Continue downhill crossing two tracks, the second one grassy and descend by three steps to a tarmac drive, where you turn left and then sharply right to join Hammer Lane and back to the pub.

· BIBLIOGRAPHY ·

Hampshire Customs, Curiosities & Country Lore — John Mann, Ensign.

Hampshire, The Complete Guide — Jo Draper, Dovecote Press.

A Hampshire Treasury — Margaret Green, Winton Publications.

Hidden Hampshire — John Barton, Countryside Books.

It Happened in Hampshire — Hampshire Women's Institutes.

The New Hampshire Village Book — Hampshire Women's Institutes.

A Picture of Hampshire — John Baker, Robert Hale.

Hampshire Treasures — Hampshire County Council.

The Surrey Village Book — Graham Collyer, Countryside Books.

Hidden Surrey — Chris Howkins, Countryside Books.

Basingstoke Canal Restoration — Jebens & Robinson, Fulltone Graphics.

English Place Names — A. D. Mills, Oxford University Press.

The Buildings of England — Pevsner & Lloyd, Penguin.

Woking to Alton Railway and Branches — V. Mitchell, Middleton.

Hampshire Railways Remembered — Robertson & Oppitz, Countryside.

In addition to the above I have made use of numerous pamphlets, parish magazines and other sources of local information.

· **ACKNOWLEDGMENTS** ·

In compiling a book of this nature, a certain amount of tolerance is required on the domestic front and I must thank my wife Phyl for enduring a profusion of maps and assorted papers scattered around during the gestation period for this book. Phyl has been as enthusiastic as I have about the book and has given me constant encouragement. I must also thank her for her companionship and support, as she accompanied me on many of the walks together with our good friend of many years, Edna Algar. Not so long ago we walked as a foursome, but now sadly, our number has been reduced to three.

Thanks also to my friend Peter Carne who has been a walking companion of mine for a few years now and has written two books of his own in this series for Ensign Publications. Peter is a veritable mine of information about Hampshire in particular and his knowledge of country life in general is deep indeed. He accompanied me on several of these walks. So I have not lacked in companionship and I am very grateful for that.

I have received much assistance from the library services of both Hampshire and Surrey in my research and a good many private people, too numerous to mention, have helped with details. I would also like to extend my thanks to the landlords, barstaffs and the customers of the public houses featured in the book, who have been enthusiastic and helpful.

This has been an entirely new sort of project for me and I am grateful to the publisher David Graves for giving me his trust and to Debbie Sermon in the office for transferring my manuscripts to disc, as well as providing me with coffee when I called!

The PUB WALKS Series

Pub Walks on the Isle of Wight

Pub Walks around the New Forest

Pub Walks in and around the New Forest

Pub Walks around Portsmouth and the South Downs

Pub Walks around Southampton and Central Hampshire

Pub Walks around Winchester and North Hampshire

Pub Walks around Basingstoke and Central Hampshire

Pub Walks around Salisbury and North Hampshire

Pub Walks around Andover and East Wiltshire

Pub Walks around Bristol and the Avon Valley

Pub Walks around Bath and the Avon Valley

Pub Walks around Oxford and the Thames Valley

Pub Walks around Chester and Wrexham

Pub Walks around Stratford-upon-Avon and Worcester

Pub Walks around Newcastle and the Tyne Valley

Pub Walks around Gloucester and Cheltenham

If you would like to contribute to this series
please submit a complete sample chapter
from your chosen area and send it to:
Ensign Publications,
2 Redcar Street,
Southampton SO1 5LL

· **Other Books** ·

Ensign publish a wide range of local history books relating to or concentrating on the Central Southern area of England.

Some recent books include:—

Hampshire Place-Names
Based on the English Place-Name Survey   Paperback   £6·95 net

The Last Flying Boat
Around the World in 50 Years   £19·95 net

"If Aeroplane had a Book of the Year this would be a strong contender"   *Aeroplane Monthly*

Fast Boats and Flying Boats
A Biography of Hubert Scott-Paine   £14·95 net

"A highly entertaining book which will also be well received by serious students of maritime and aviation history. Compulsive reading."   *Motor Boat and Yachting*

Great Steamers White and Gold
An Illustrated History of Royal Mail Ships and Services   £24·95 net

The Strange Death of King William Rufus
A New Forest Mystery   Paperback   £4·95 net

The Bovington Tank Collection
Including Other Armoured Fighting Vehicles   Paperback   £14·95 net

The County Murders Series

Dorset Murders   Paperback   £6·95 net

Hampshire Murders   Paperback   £6·95 net

Sussex Murders   Paperback   £6·95 net

If you have difficulty ordering any of these books from your local bookshop please ring us on 0703 702639 and we will supply you by post — but please do try your local bookshop first.